Careers in Banking and Finance

Careers in Banking and Finance

FOURTH EDITION

DAVID SNELGAR

KOGAN PAGE
CAREERS
SERIES

Acknowledgements

When revising *Careers in Banking and Finance* I drew heavily upon the careers and recruitment literature put out by banks and other institutions mentioned in this book and upon the publications of the Banking Information Service. In addition to the employees whose case studies I have been permitted to use, I should like to thank the following who all found time to talk to me and/or to read and comment on relevant parts of the text: Sheila Bentham of the Banking Information Service; Julian Bishop of the Bank of England; Jim Tucker of the Halifax Building Society; Lindsay Hanson, Kleinwort Benson; and Peter Welch, Credit Card Research Group. I am grateful to all those who took the trouble to answer my queries by letter or by telephone, especially David Ledger, Finance & Leasing Association; Brian Rawle and Chris Moon, Chartered Institute of Bankers; and Neil Matthewson, London Investment Banking Association. I am especially indebted to Julia Allen, author of the earlier editions of this book, on whose work I have relied very heavily, and to my wife, Gill, for her patience during the preparation of this edition.

First published in 1988, by Julia Allen
Second edition 1989
Third edition 1992
Fourth edition 1995, by David Snelgar
Reprinted with revisions 1996

Kogan Page Limited
120 Pentonville Road
London N1 9JN

British Library Cataloguing in Publication Data

A CIP record for this book is available from the British Library.

ISBN 0-7494-1552-5

Typeset by DP Photosetting, Aylesbury, Bucks
Printed and bound in Great Britain by
Clays Ltd, St Ives plc

Contents

Foreword

I am pleased to have the opportunity to write the foreword to this book. I visit many schools and colleges and am aware of the genuine interest of pupils in banking and in careers within the financial services sector.

The banks are anxious to provide as much information as possible to young people about the world of finance, and their staff, and the speakers from the Banking Information Service Bankers' Panel, which represents the clearing banks, visit schools throughout the country with the aim of providing first-hand information and guidance to students and teachers at careers conventions and during careers classes.

In any talk it is impossible to convey more than a general impression of the work and responsibilities involved. With such a varied scene, it is difficult to do more than stimulate an interest in such a complex, rapidly changing and fascinating subject.

This book has a wide application and provides valuable information and help to those seeking a career in the world of finance. Banking offers a worthwhile career and the effort to achieve success is very rewarding.

Sheila Bentham
Banking Information Service
1994

Introduction

The financial world is still going through a period of profound change: institutions are restructuring; recruiting and training policies are being modified in view of the need to reduce the size of the workforce; new technology is affecting working methods; competition between sectors increases. This has made it difficult to obtain reliable, up-to-date information. I must, therefore, warn readers that, although the information I have supplied was to the best of my knowledge true at the time of writing (1994), it could very quickly become out of date and I would advise them to check it at source.

In the mid-1980s there was a considerable interest in jobs connected with money management, and stories about very high salaries earned by very young money market dealers were common. It seemed that almost everyone wanted to work in the City of London, and to get rich quick. Then came the slump of 1987, and belts were tightened; many of those who were said to have earned 'telephone number' salaries became unemployed. This book does not attempt to describe the exceptional opportunities or hazards; it is a guide for those looking for a business sector where they might spend their entire working lives.

When you say the words 'banking and finance' to people you will nearly always get a reaction: some yawn at their mere mention, for others the phrase carries an aura of sinister glamour. Few, however, have any notion of what it really means. Many of the people in post whom I spoke to said, 'I'd no idea what would be involved', 'I'd never given banking or finance a thought', 'It never occurred to me that I'd be able to cope with the work' or 'I was never any good at maths'. But there they were, people from widely differing backgrounds, all coping with and enjoying the work. Some had been drawn to it because it seemed to promise security and attractive fringe benefits, others liked the team work and customer contact, and those in career posts welcomed the intellectual challenge, the responsibility they shouldered, and the opportunities for promotion on merit, not length of service.

The Banks

Banking in the UK has a long history, but no one who has looked at a modern cheque book or bank statement could fail to see that banking has moved with the times. Some people's only contact with their bank is a brief exchange with a cashier as they make a deposit or withdraw money from their current account, but even these people must suspect that there is very much more to banking than this. Next time you are in a bank, pick up a set of leaflets describing the different services on offer; you will be surprised at their range and will soon realise that cashiering is only one - albeit an important one - of a great variety of tasks performed by bank employees.

The banks that we as private account holders know are the high street banks[1] and they, of course, also handle business accounts. But there are the merchant banks, now often referred to as investment banks, the finance houses, the international and foreign banks and the Bank of England, the Government's bank, all of which recruit school-leavers and graduates. There are chapters devoted to all these different institutions.

The Building Societies

The building societies are as familiar a part of the high street scene as the banks. They used to be concerned exclusively with providing their customers with savings and mortgage facilities, but with the passing of the Building Societies Act the range of their work has widened and their traditional image is changing; there is now a considerable overlap between the areas in which building societies and banks operate.

[1] Their more technical name is the clearing banks. Clearing is the process of passing a cheque from the bank where it has been paid in, through the central clearing system, to the bank where it has been drawn; and the cheque is said to have cleared when the drawer's account has been debited; the process takes three business days.

Entering a Profession

You should be quite clear that when you join the staff of a bank or a building society you will be joining a profession and one which still retains a hierarchy of posts. Although, in common with many other organisations, the pyramid of promotion has considerably flattened, there remain opportunities to progress on merit to more senior posts. Your development will be assisted by obtaining relevant professional qualifications, not only of banking, but of insurance, investment and other disciplines. Some people get it into their heads when they are at school that they are no good at exams and vow that, once they have left, they will never take another. Quite a number of such people, after they have been in a job for a while and found that they are interested in and good at the work, change their minds, decide to study for the professional examinations and, to their great surprise, sail through them. Whether you are a natural exam taker or, in this respect, a late developer, you will be given every opportunity and encouragement at work to acquire professional or vocational qualifications. There are chapters on professional qualifications and the institutes that award them. However, it must be said that success at exams is not the sole criterion used in the selection of people for top posts.

The Qualities Required

Banks, building societies and other financial institutions handle money; their employees, while they do not have to possess great mathematical gifts, must be numerate. Most of the calculations are done by machines, but those who operate the machines need a feel for figures and GCSE (or equivalent) mathematics is desirable.[2] The work also calls for a methodical approach, accuracy and attention to detail. Those applying for a career post may imagine they will not be expected to type (indeed they won't be, though typing is always a useful skill), but almost everyone who works in a financial institution of any kind uses a VDU so you *will* have to get to grips with the technology and learn your way round the QWERTY keyboard.

[2] Note: throughout the book the formula GCSE/A level (or equivalent) has been used in order to avoid repeating every time GCSE, SCE, H grade etc. If you are in any doubt about the equivalence of your academic qualifications ask your school careers teacher or college or university careers adviser, or write to the personnel department of the institution in which you are interested.

There seem to be few jobs nowadays which do not require 'good communication skills' - the phrase has become a cliché - but in the context of the jobs described in this book, what does it mean? All sections of the population use banks and building societies and some of the regulations governing financial transactions are complicated. You might find yourself explaining to a pensioner the advantages of opening a savings account, interviewing a young couple who want to buy their first house, or telling a company about trading conditions in Tokyo. Knowing the subject is not enough; you must also be able to enlighten the uninitiated and hold your own with the experts. Your supervisors will be assessing how well you deal with the public because customers tend to judge a bank or a building society by the performance of its contact staff.

Intense competition in the financial sector is leading individual banks to look for marketing and sales staff who have commercial awareness and who are able to think creatively. All staff, whether or not they deal directly with the public, are expected to identify opportunities to sell products and services, and those who are in the front line will find that selling is an integral part of their job.

Clothes and appearance also make an impression on customers: staff will be expected to dress in suitable office attire, and many institutions now issue staff with a uniform, or clothing from a corporate catalogue especially designed for the personnel of that organisation.

Most important of all are the character traits needed for these professions. You will be handling people's money and be privy to a lot of confidential information. All staff have to be honest, trustworthy and discreet and to demonstrate a sense of responsibility - in other words, possess complete professional integrity.

Conditions of Employment

What attracts you to banking or building society work will depend on the sort of person you are. There are some who want nothing more than a job and, indeed, the pay and hours compare favourably with those of other kinds of office work, the premises are pleasant and the fringe benefits good. Others demand challenge, rapid advancement and high financial rewards and, if they are of the right calibre, that is what they will find.

The high street banks and national building societies are huge institutions with staffs of many thousands. You may start at an office near to your home, possibly a local customer services branch which may have fewer than ten employees, or perhaps a processing centre supporting a number of local offices. During your career you must be prepared to move offices - not just once, but several times. You will be expected to gain experience in a number of branches, and perhaps do a stint in the regional office responsible for controlling the development of many dozen branches in that sector of the country. Certainly you should not expect to spend your entire working life within walking distance of your home. If you are attracted to the work but not to the idea of mobility, you may wish to base yourself in London, or in a major provincial city, and apply to a London-based bank without a large branch network, or to a building society or finance house operating within a limited geographical area.

The Benefits

Salaries are usually reviewed annually, and rises depend on performance. Staff in some areas, including London, are paid a territorial allowance. New employees are normally given a minimum of 21 working days' paid holiday each year, and as your years of service rise, so will your leave entitlement, up to a level of 30 days or more. Established career staff are granted quite generous sick pay terms in the event of protracted illness. Most institutions allow study leave and some contribute to the cost of tuition fees and books. Other benefits will probably include membership of a contributory or non-contributory company pension scheme, an annual bonus and/or a profit-sharing scheme, low interest loan and mortgage facilities, and help with house removal costs if you are moved at your employer's request.

Employment Outlook

The High Street Banks

At the time of writing recruitment numbers are considerably lower than they were in the late 1980s. Not only has the economic climate resulted in public demand for banking services growing more slowly, but a programme of mergers and branch closures, and investment in IT (information technology) have all reduced the total numbers employed in the financial services industry. It is, of course, impossible to say how long this will last but the major banks have continued a policy of graduate selection throughout the difficult years, and a number of institutions are now resuming general recruitment of school/college leavers, albeit cautiously. Opportunities also arise when a new administration or computer centre is set up which cannot be staffed from existing personnel. However, much of the recruitment at present consists of fixed-term contracts of one or two years. It is too soon to judge how many of these contracts will be extended, and how many on such contracts will join the permanent staff, although some are already being offered this opportunity. Senior bankers have gone on record as saying that staff can no longer assume employment from the cradle to the grave. But as the programme of early retirement and staff reduction eases off, and staff numbers stabilise, so will a pattern of career development and promotion for staff once again appear, and the beneficiaries will include the more promising of non-graduate recruits.

Girobank

Having gone through a time of expansion in 1988/9 Girobank is now in a period of consolidation. In 1994 it was not actively recruiting people for clerical grades; you should check the up-to-date position with a regional office.

The Department for National Savings

In common with many organisations, numbers employed have fallen in recent years. National Savings recruit direct for staff when vacancies arise, and advertise in the local and national press.

The Building Societies

Many societies have recruited no additional staff since 1990, but in late 1994 they reported a resumption of selective recruitment for local vacancies. The larger societies have a limited programme to recruit management trainees, and certain employers are expanding staffing at centralised locations which will serve their network of branches.

In Part I of this book there is information about the different employers – the Bank of England, the high street banks, merchant banks, finance houses, international banks, Girobank, the Department for National Savings and the building societies – and a chapter on getting a job. In Part 2 there is information on professional bodies, qualifications and courses, addresses and recommended reading.

Part 1

Chapter 1

The Bank of England

Introduction

As the central bank of the United Kingdom, the Bank of England is at the core of the UK financial system. Given the open nature of the UK economy, the strength of the UK financial sector and London's prominence as a financial centre, the Bank also plays a major international role.

The Bank of England's overriding objective is a stable financial framework for the effective functioning and development of the economy. The Bank of England has three core purposes and derives its many activities from them. They are

- the maintenance of the integrity and value of the currency;
- the maintenance of the integrity of the financial system;
- the promotion of the efficiency and effectiveness of UK financial services.

Monetary Stability

Underpinning this objective is a firm commitment to achieving price stability, and the view that monetary policy should be directed to that end. As part of the Government's move to enhance the degree of public scrutiny of policy making in this vital area, the Bank now publishes its independent quarterly *Inflation Report*. It is against the projections of inflation developed for that report that monetary policy advice is given to the Treasury.

Central banks are at the heart of each country's financial system because they can influence the liquidity of the system. The Bank implements monetary policy by setting the terms, particularly the interest rates, on which that liquidity is provided to the financial markets. Its operations influence interest rates in the economy at large, and the exchange rate.

The Bank also manages the country's gold and foreign

exchange reserves, and can influence exchange rates directly by intervening in the exchange markets to buy or sell sterling for foreign currencies.

The Bank also manages the Government's operations in bond markets - notably in the gilt-edged market - selling Government securities to fund the Public Sector Borrowing Requirement.

The Bank of England as a bank

Not only involved in policy matters, the Bank also provides banking services to its customers, principally the Government, the banking system, and other central banks. It plays a key role in the principal payment and settlement systems to improve money transmissions and acts as a bank of issue, producing and distributing $5\frac{1}{2}$ million banknotes each day.

Financial stability

The Bank has an explicit statutory responsibility for the supervision of banking institutions that take deposits from the public in this country, with the objective of protecting depositors. The Bank also has formal responsibility for supervising the firms in the wholesale markets for sterling, foreign exchange and bullion. Financial markets have been changing rapidly and this has made the task of supervision more complex and challenging. The Bank's supervisory and surveillance teams have been strengthened, with an increased emphasis on being alert to signs of possible criminality, on the assessment of trading risks, and on surveillance of developments in banks' home countries which could have implications for financial stability in the UK. Globalisation of financial markets has increased the international dimension of supervision.

Efficient and competitive markets

London is the leading financial centre in Europe. The Bank works to ensure that London has the necessary infrastructure to maintain this position, monitoring its development and identifying weaknesses and competitive threats. Among the priorities in this area are ensuring the security and efficiency of payment and settlement systems, assessing the impact on the financial sector of European legislation and promoting more efficient forms of corporate finance.

The structure of the Bank

The figure below gives the Bank's structure in more detail.

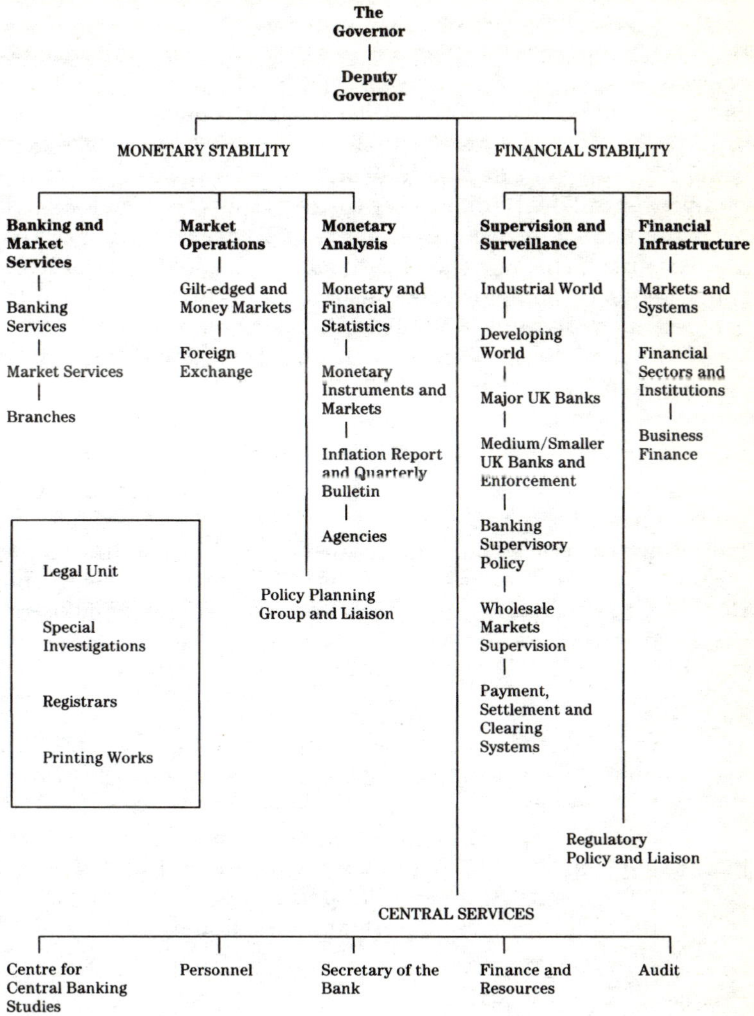

Getting a Job with the Bank

There are three levels of entry: GCSE (or equivalent), A level (or equivalent), graduate and postgraduate. If you are thinking of applying, you should write in November to the Bank's Personnel Division for an application form.

GCSE (or equivalent) Entrants

Ideally, applicants at this level will have had a broadly based education and will show an aptitude for figures and written work. The Bank receives a lot of applications, but only a few of those who apply are interviewed; it is therefore very important to present yourself well on the application form and to fill it in carefully and accurately. References will be requested from your school and from anyone who has employed you. Interviews generally last about half an hour and take the form of a friendly two-way chat. The Bank will try to get to know you, but you will have the chance to ask questions and, as you can reveal a lot about yourself through the questions you ask, it is a good idea to think about these before the interview. As interviews are held before you take your GCSE examinations, you will be given a series of written tests designed to establish your suitability for employment by the Bank.

Training

The Bank usually takes on a number of recruits at the same time - it is easier for them to settle in that way - and in their first few days they are given a short induction course. Most of the training is given on the job by someone who is already doing the work, but the Bank has its own training centre and during your first year you will attend a two-day familiarisation course.

The Work

There are many different jobs for entrants at this level, but first jobs are likely to be in the Banking and Market Services Division, the Central Services Division, or the Monetary Analysis Division. You could find yourself helping to operate a computer system, using a keyboard and VDU, processing documents and checking their accuracy, recording and filing information, answering the telephone, taking messages or dealing with queries.

Prospects

The jobs you undertake, the responsibility you acquire and the promotion you gain will depend upon your ability and performance. You will be a member of a huge organisation, but it is one in which no one is forgotten or overlooked. Four times during your first year, and at least once a year thereafter, you will see your supervisor or manager in order to talk over your performance in the previous period and your plans for the next.

Case Study
Jenny[1] works in the Monetary and Financial Statistics Section.

> When I get out my Bank of England cheque book to pay for something, I always get a few raised eyebrows. People are impressed. I like the old building, the marble, the mosaics, the doormen in their pink coats, but then I like tradition. I don't want it to change, not on the outside at any rate. Inside, of course, it is very modern. I don't expect people think of Bank of England staff spending much of the day in front of a VDU, but that's a lot of what I do. I deal with more than 300 different international banks, checking for errors and putting the statistical information on to the computer. It's mostly figure work, but then I'm happy dealing with figures. The work was quite hard when I first joined, but people are very helpful and because they work with you, you soon learn. I seem to spend a lot of time on the phone clearing up mistakes. Many of my contacts are in foreign banks and speak little English. The challenge is getting through the language barrier to get the information you need.

A-level (or equivalent) Entrants

The Bank is looking for people who have had a good all-round education and whose GCSE (or equivalent) passes include English language and mathematics. Applicants at this level should have, or be studying for, at least two academic A-level subjects. At your interview you will be given the chance to show whether or not you are friendly, hard working, able to work in a team, a good communicator and can apply your intelligence to a wide range of problems.

Training

On your first day you will attend an induction course, but you will receive most of your basic training on the job from people already doing the work. During your early years you will probably be sent on two or three separate training courses within the Bank.

The Work

A-level entrants usually begin in one of the following areas: the Banking and Market Services Division, the Financial Statistics Division, or the Central Services Division. In their first years they build up a wide range of experience by undertaking a number of very different jobs. To begin with, much of your work will be

[1] The case studies in this chapter are quoted with permission from the Bank of England's recruitment literature.

confined to the day-to-day operational activities of the Bank but it will be demanding and satisfying.

Prospects

The Bank has a staff appraisal system and promotion is entirely on merit. The Bank will provide support for relevant study courses. That support is conditional upon good performance.

Case Study

Jane joined the bank two-and-a-half years ago with A levels in physics, chemistry, maths and further maths. She is now in the Clearing Centre.

> Ten jobs in two-and-a-half years, how's that for variety? When I joined the Bank I went straight into the Clearing Centre. This is an area which 'clears' all the many thousands of cheques which come into the Bank each day. These include cheques drawn on other banks as well as cheques drawn on the Bank of England by such organisations as the Inland Revenue, Customs and Excise, and Paymaster General, and our own bank staff. Up to a quarter of a million cheques may be processed here each day and we're dealing in hundreds of millions of pounds.
>
> Two months after arriving here, I was made a team leader helping and showing others how to do the job. I didn't expect to get responsibility like that quite so soon. It wasn't easy, being so new, but it was excellent training in motivating staff.
>
> Six months later the whole section moved to a brand new office with a more up-to-date computer system. Since then I've been continually on the move. The best job was in the accounting section where I acted as a settlements clerk. Here we agreed the overall figures which we should pay different banks and they should pay us. We worked to very strict deadlines under considerable pressure and always dealing in large sums. It was challenging, stretching and enjoyable.
>
> What next? I've just passed all the necessary aptitude tests to have a stab at becoming a foreign exchange dealer. There are real opportunities in the Bank if you're prepared to work and prove your ability.

Graduate and Postgraduate Entrants

Typically, the Bank takes on between 25 and 35 entrants at this level every year; it is looking for people possessing the intellectual and personal qualities that will enable them to fill analytical, advisory and managerial positions. The Bank seeks to recruit intellectual excellence and lively characters in whatever discipline it can find them. In addition to their academic qualifications, applicants should possess good communication skills and be able to work on their own initiative and as a member of a team. If you are applying while still at university, the careers advisory service will let you know the recruiting visit dates. Direct applications from those who have left university are welcome. In recent years, a number of posts have been filled on a contract basis from second-jobbers.

Training

There is a modular Trainee Officials Programme which takes place during the first four years after entry. Courses provide entrants with a general introduction to the Bank's operations and enable them to build up a broad understanding of management within the Bank. Some are at the Bank's training centre and others are designed to equip them with specific technical skills. There are opportunities for secondment to outside bodies such as merchant banks, international financial organisations and government departments.

The Work

You will be assigned to a post right away and will be expected to make a significant contribution early on. You will probably remain in the area of your first posting for about three years, where you may work in more than one job. Most people will move to a new area after three years or so.

Prospects

Promotion is entirely on merit and people of outstanding ability can rise very rapidly.

Case Study

Neeta joined the Bank six years ago with a first degree in Accounting and Law. She works in the Financial Stability Wing.

> I have developed my career in a variety of roles within the financial stability area. Initially working in Payment, Settlement and Clearing Systems, I have carried out research into various issues affecting banking practice at that time, including the implications of drug trafficking, and money laundering legislation. I then went on to be part of the team responsible for setting up a new screen-based settlement system for money market instruments, specialising in the legal aspects of the project. This was followed by three years' experience in Supervision.

I was supervising a number of small and medium-sized UK banks - a role which demanded a large degree of technical knowledge and was made all the more interesting as this was when a small number of banks found themselves in difficulty.

I have just been appointed Personal Assistant to the Deputy Director responsible for supervision and surveillance, and I am also Secretary to the Board of Banking Supervision.

I'm providing support to the Deputy Director across a wide range of his responsibilities, anticipating his requirements and being ready to deal with a whole variety of tasks as they arise. It's early days yet and, while my supervision experience is very useful in enabling me to understand many of the issues, there's a vast amount to learn, particularly on the surveillance side. The pace is incredibly hectic and I couldn't begin to say how many things come up in a day. But it's an invaluable opportunity to get a view from the top, and see how the Bank interacts with other organisations at a high level.

I have to juggle my responsibilities as PA with those of Secretary to the Board of Banking Supervision: the Board comprises members from outside the Bank, meets monthly, and advises on issues facing banking supervisors. This is primarily an administrative role and one which complements my job as PA, giving me a special insight into the priority issues facing the Board.

Conditions of Employment and Benefits

Trainee Scale

All entrants to the Bank spend their first year as trainee bank officers. There are minimum salaries for junior clerical, A-level and graduate entrants, but salaries are not age-related. Management has the flexibility to offer salaries above the specified minimum. After completion of one year's service, progression will depend on factors such as performance and an assessment of an individual's ability.

Place of Work

The Bank's head office is in Threadneedle Street in the heart of the City; it has other premises within 'the Square Mile', branches in a number of provincial centres and an office in Glasgow. The Printing Works are at Loughton in Essex; the Registrar's Department is in Gloucester; and there is a recreation centre at Roehampton.

Further Information

General information on the Bank may be obtained from the

Public Enquiries Group: application forms and recruitment literature are obtainable from the Recruitment Section, Personnel Division (address on p. 99).

Chapter 2

The High Street Banks

Introduction

The high street (or clearing) banks are, as the term suggests, very much part of the everyday scene and practically everyone, at some stage in his or her life, has a bank account. There are branches throughout the country and they conduct four-fifths of Britain's banking business. These banks offer their customers a wide range of services and the career opportunities open to their staff are correspondingly varied. Many customers simply use a bank as a secure place to keep their money and confine their operations to depositing and withdrawing funds, but for those who wish, the bank will pay regularly recurring bills, issue foreign currency, travellers' cheques and credit cards, arrange travel or general insurance, provide mortgages, buy and sell shares, supply secure storage for documents and articles of value, grant loans and overdrafts, provide investment and tax advice, offer life assurance and pensions planning, handle documentation and provide payment services for international trade, assist with drawing up a will, and act as executor or trustee; all of these services require trained and experienced staff.

The high street banks are The Bank of Scotland, Barclays Bank, Clydesdale Bank, The Co-operative Bank, Lloyds Bank, Midland Bank, National Westminster Bank, The Royal Bank of Scotland, TSB Bank, Yorkshire Bank, and Abbey National. They are very good at promoting their services and, in addition, all produce excellent free illustrated careers literature. It would be a good idea to write off for some of this (addresses on pp. 99–100) in order to learn what individual banks say about themselves, because in this chapter we shall concentrate on the points they have in common. Coutts & Co (a subsidiary of National Westminster) describes itself as a private bank and offers services to a particular customer group. As such, Coutts should be contacted direct about career opportunities, as much of what is written here is not applicable.

All the banks are experimenting with different ways to serve their customers, making use of developing technology. Some offer links with their customers' home- or office-based computers; other units provide a total banking service by telephone, of which the longest established is Midland's First Direct, available 24 hours a day throughout the year (including bank holidays). The staff working at such centres are usually recruited locally and your careers officer will advise you of any employers based near your home.

If you are still at school, you can sometimes get an idea of what it is like to work in a bank by joining a work experience programme. Your careers teacher should know which banks in your area offer placements.

Most bank staff begin their careers in a branch of one of the high street banks and if you are an A-level or GCSE entrant, or equivalent, you will probably join one of the banks in your local community. Jobs are graded according to their difficulty and to the amount of responsibility they carry and most people, whatever their qualifications, begin in the training grade, usually called Grade One. Most banks have special entry grade schemes for graduates.

The Clerical Grades

Historically, most banks had four or five basic clerical grades, some appointed grades (called assistant manager, or similar), and a number of managerial grades. In several banks this picture is changing, with a pattern of fewer grades at clerical and managerial levels, a wider range of responsibilities within each grade, and longer spent in each role, resulting in more experienced staff providing a higher standard of service to customers. But for the purpose of this book I have used the established grading structure which is only now starting to be modified.

Grade One

In this training grade you receive a grounding in the basics of banking, you learn office procedures and are introduced to a computer terminal. You may start these duties at a branch, or at a regional processing centre, handling the back-office work of voucher and data processing for a number of branches, all served with a regular document collection service by van or courier.

Every office is linked to the bank's main computer system, from which the terminal operators obtain customer information such as account balances, and enter details of counter transactions such as cheques cashed and funds deposited into accounts. Every working day all those cheques paid in at the branch, which are drawn on accounts of other branches and banks, are remitted through the central clearing system to the branch or bank holding that account. Nearly all customers' statements are now despatched direct to customers from a main printing and mailing centre, but you will handle those statements which have been returned to the account-holding office for the inclusion of additional paperwork, such as dividend vouchers. Quite early on you will be dealing with customers' telephone enquiries. Although much of this work is repetitive and demands attention to detail as it has to be done accurately, there is enough variety to make it interesting and you will be working as part of a team. You are also expected to be alive to opportunities for selling additional services to your customers.

Grade Two

Within this grade, branch-based staff will probably have their first face-to-face contact with customers, which for many people is the most rewarding aspect of the work. Cashiering is an important job because, to a large extent, a bank is judged by the performance of its counter staff. When the banking hall is full a cashier can be under considerable pressure, but must at all times remain polite and unflustered and work quickly and accurately, looking out for irregular transactions and for possible attempted frauds. Grade Two duties may also include maintaining cash dispenser machines and issuing cash cards, reception and enquiries work, processing standing orders and attending to related correspondence. Customers ask the bank to make regular payments by standing order or direct debit on their behalf for such things as insurance premiums, mortgage payments, and regular household utility bills. Any changes to these instructions must be entered as computer data. In Grade Two the emphasis on selling awareness is equally important; as an example, enquiries and counter staff will be expected to promote their bank's credit and cash cards, or telephone banking services in appropriate cases.

Case Study

Kate has a Grade Two post in a clearing bank. The work which she describes takes place in a traditional banking branch. Increasingly banks are centralising much of their processing work at operations centres serving a number of branches within several miles radius, relieving the branch staff of paperwork, and leaving them free to concentrate on helping their customers face-to-face. Nevertheless, the work which Kate describes will be familiar to bank staff both in the traditional and in the modern customer service branches.

I took my A levels but failed them, which is why I didn't go to university. After my A-level results came through, I wrote on spec to all the banks just asking if they had any jobs, rather than looking through the papers.

When I started I had to do what they called a 'programmed learning course'. Some years ago it was on tape but now all the banks use interactive videos which is much more interesting and helps your concentration.

My first job was in the accounts section, or 'machine room', and it was sorting vouchers into order. It was very boring. I must admit my reaction when I got home on my first day was: 'I don't want to do this for the rest of my life!' At the same time you're trained on the machines. At first, although I could use a keyboard – I can type and I'd played the piano – I felt so slow and I thought I'd never get anywhere at all, but I picked up speed quickly and got confidence and it got better then. In those days it was 11 months before I met customers, but it happens much quicker now. You need the background you get in the machine room, you've got to know your accounts, but I was dying to get down to the general office. In the general office I started off on a job called 'returns'; this is returning cheques. I did the paperwork; it was a two-person job. I had much more responsibility than in the machine room and I enjoyed that job very much. Then I moved on to the enquiries counter, handling people's cheque books and statements and printouts, and the other part of the job was sending out customers' statements. I like meeting customers. I'd had phone contact with them on the returns job. In fact, at the enquiries counter the situation is: 'Can I have a printout, please?' or 'Can I have a cheque book?' and that's it, really, except that I am now expected to sell some of our services to my customers. You don't have an awful lot of contact except with the people who come in every day. You have a little chat with them and get to know them quite well which is nice.

I began to take the banking exams, but exams were never my strong point. When I started I got day-release. I got through the first stage but it's a long course. You can get quite far without exams, even up to managerial level.

I've been at the same branch ever since I started, five-and-a-half years ago. Most of my friends from school went to university and many of them are still looking for a job. One friend, with a history degree behind her, is temping. I'm glad I didn't go to university because I have got much more experience in a job. Banking is reasonably well paid and you've got quite a few perks: after you reach a certain age you get a good mortgage rate, you have better interest rates on loans, you get a Christmas bonus, an annual pay review and profit sharing each year.

The thing I like best is customer contact. One of the things I did was to help run a sub-branch. We were out in a village and there were just two staff and that meant a lot of customer contact and a lot of variety. As it was the only bank in the village people came in and asked all sorts of questions. If I didn't know the answers I contacted the main branch. I was getting a lot of experience out there. I was there for 18 months and thoroughly enjoyed it because I got to know the customers.

I'm what's called a customer service officer now. I'm opening and closing accounts, I'm doing paperwork, I see a few customers and talk to them over the phone. I'm in Grade Two at the moment. Hopefully, in the next few months, I'll be in for a supervisor's job and they are Grade Three.

Grades Three and Four

When you reach these grades you will be introduced to foreign work: buying and selling foreign currency and travellers' cheques, helping customers who trade overseas to settle their accounts, arranging insurance applications and obtaining information on trading conditions in foreign markets.

You will do securities work: safeguarding the money the bank lends to its customers, that is making sure that the security – which might be the deeds of a house, an endowment insurance policy, a third party guarantee or stocks and shares – is in order; buying and selling stocks and shares on behalf of customers; and arranging for the safe custody of valuables in the bank's strongroom. You will supervise the work of the cheque remittance team and the terminal operators – remember it will not be so long ago that you were doing this work – and you will spend some time as a manager's assistant, answering routine correspondence, marketing the bank's services, agreeing to small loans and overdrafts and helping the manager to assess loan requests and arrange securities. In these roles you will spend most of your time dealing directly with customers, advising them on their personal or business banking, and marketing the bank's products and services.

Case Study

Sally, now a Grade Four officer, joined a high street bank at the age of 16 with four O levels.

> When I was going to leave school and thought I should be looking for a job, I wrote round to all the banks. Banking seemed a secure job to go for, but I didn't really have any idea what was involved. I thought it was just paying in and cashing cheques, but I soon found out that it's vastly different. Some people employed in a bank don't even deal with cash.
>
> I started off in the accounts section - most juniors start there. It's general duties: sending out customers' statements, answering the telephone and processing all the work through a computer. On your first day they give you a set of manuals to read, new entrants' manuals, which are very useful; they give you all the background information and you read them as you do the job. It's a teach-yourself method, but all banks now have induction courses for entrants. And when you start to use a computer you teach yourself. You sit at the machine and it tells you what to do and when you give an answer, it tells you whether it's right or wrong. They don't let you loose on customers right away, obviously you have to build up your background knowledge, but you get your first customer contact quite early on. The machine room has a supervisor and I went on to help her and then I was moved to the counter for general cashiering. I really enjoyed that as there's a lot of customer contact. After general cashiering I did foreign cashiering and a bit of securities work and then became a receptionist, or personal banker. Receptionists are there purely to talk to customers and help them with any problem, point them in the right direction and, for something like lending, put them in touch with someone higher up.
>
> I've been on training courses and I really enjoyed that. Recently they've been very hard work, but you get a lot from them, they're very helpful. They last a week, or a couple of weeks; you stay at a residential training centre, or sometimes a local hotel and you meet people from all over the country.
>
> Last September I was transferred to the local regional office to be an instructor. There are several of us and we give courses. These last for anything from two to four days. There might be four or six different subjects and we take it in turns to give talks to the students. For the rest of the day, when we're not instructing, we're back in the personnel department doing background work for the courses and all the administration - there's a lot of administration.
>
> I've been here nine-and-a-half years now and I've reached Grade Four. Although I haven't taken any of the banking exams, I'm keen to get on; I'm in my twenties and established in an interesting career.

These are the so-called clerical grades and everyone works his or her way through them, but the speed at which you do this depends on you, on how well you perform and on the qualifications with which you joined the bank. Although you can reach this level without having to pass any banking exams, there is an increasing emphasis on staff obtaining relevant qualifications, particularly if they are involved in advising customers on pensions or investments.

Entry Requirements

It may be possible to join some high street banks even without formal academic qualifications; the banks place great importance on personal qualities which include getting on with other people, being an effective communicator, mixing well in a team, and being enthusiastic and ambitious. Experience of other work such as a Saturday job, and what you have achieved outside the classroom will all help your application.

Most bank employees start work at the age of 18 when they leave school or college. Since the early 1990s most clearing banks have restricted their non-graduate recruitment to short-term contracts of one or two years. However, there are signs that some of those employees may be offered permanent appointments when their contracts are due for renewal. Banks differ in the academic qualifications they ask for; while some do not specify any minimum qualifications, others like their staff to be educated to GCSE (or equivalent) standard and for their passes to include English and mathematics. If you have A levels (or equivalent) and are considered to have management potential, you might be selected for an accelerated training programme.

A degree in any academic subject can be the entrée to a management training scheme; some degree subjects, eg law, economics, business and management studies or statistics, can be useful and it is particularly helpful if you are fluent in more than one language. A very high standard of performance is demanded of graduates and they are expected to absorb in a matter of months what others can take years to learn.

Case Study

Graeme, now a Grade Four Securities Officer in a high street bank, entered as a graduate trainee.

> I have a joint honours degree in French and English and I decided vaguely that I'd try to get into the financial services. Simply by reading

about the options that were open I felt it might be an interesting path to pursue.

I joined a graduate trainee programme, which is an accelerated training scheme. However, beyond that there are a series of internal courses, where you are assessed on work that you have undertaken during the course and your own performance in a particular branch and, depending on your results, either you are pushed on at a faster rate than people in your group or slowed down, but you have to meet the required standard as you progress.

I've been with the bank just over three years and I've completed the basic training comprising the clerical duties, such as working on the counter - cashiering, processing cheques, that sort of thing. Latterly, in the past year-and-a-half to two years, I've spent some time dealing with the corporate side of foreign work, for example dealing with exporting and importing, negotiating bills etc, then on to what we call securities work, which obviously covers the taking of security to cover loans that the bank makes. More recently I've been working as a manager's assistant, which is similar to a PA to a particular manager.

I've taken all the banking exams, which were a significant challenge. I had to master subjects - accountancy and law - that were new to me, but I think I got through because I'd learnt how to apply myself academically at university. At this point in time I don't know exactly where I'll end up. I have broad ideas about areas I'd like to move into and really, at this stage, I'm hoping to gain an overview of the different sectors of the bank in order to make some sort of cogent decision as to which way I'll go in the end.

I enjoy working with people, customers and people in the branch, helping customers articulate their problems in financial terms, reaching compromises or solutions, meeting customer needs. I also find the financial world interesting, it stimulates me intellectually and in many other ways. I find there is more interest within the financial sector than I had originally imagined. I think it has diversified significantly in the last five years or so and will continue to do so and I feel that it offers opportunities across the board. You don't have to end up a Lending Manager, which might have been the case 20 years ago; you can work in virtually any department within the group and it's such a wide group that you have scope for all sorts of creative fulfilment.

Initially, I was worried that I hadn't followed any course that was linked with banking or finance, that I hadn't any numeracy skills that I knew about. I wasn't sure that I'd have the intuitive ability to function in this type of environment. I think my biggest worry was that I would not be able to match the requirements of the job. But you can learn a certain amount and I think a certain amount is derived through day-to-day contact with people in similar situations and, of course, through work experience. On a graduate training scheme you have to pass through the different stages of the job with minimal training and a very short time is spent on a particular function. You have only a superficial look at a piece of work and then go on to the next stage, so you have to be able to extract the information you require and apply it very quickly. Everyone reaches their own level and, at this stage, it's difficult to see what mine will be. There is scope within the bank to reach a high level of seniority and that may take you virtually the full span of your career. On the other hand, you could end up in a fairly senior position at the age of, say, 40 and if you'd reached the level of your own abilities you'd be happy in that position.

Training

All banks provide excellent training which will continue throughout your career. Most of the training for the clerical posts is one-to-one, on-the-job training given by someone who is fully trained and already doing the work, but this is supplemented by courses at the bank's training centre and in-house branch courses. The banks also use self-instructional video and computer-aided training kits, which have the advantage of allowing you to work at your own pace. At all stages your performance will be assessed and you will have the chance to discuss your progress with one of your superiors or with the personnel officer.

Some of the high street banks offer sponsorship or bursary schemes to undergraduates studying relevant degree courses. These usually incorporate a sandwich or gap year placement with the bank, and guarantee the opportunity to reach the final stages of that bank's graduate selection scheme. Packages offered by individual banks change quite regularly so you should obtain details of what is currently on offer direct from the Banking Information Service (address on p. 99).

Professional Qualifications

Not all entrants join the bank with their eyes on a career, although this is expected of graduate trainees. Many people are happy to remain in the clerical grades: the work is varied and carries a certain amount of responsibility, there is customer contact and the satisfaction of working in a team, and the pay is reasonable. Some will specialise in selling insurance or investment services from an early stage, and within those fields there are promotion opportunities. However, for others, the challenging and interesting work begins beyond the clerical grades and to get there it is helpful to pass professional examinations. For most staff there will be the qualifications of the Chartered Institute of Bankers or the Chartered Institute of Bankers in Scotland, details of which are set out in Chapters 11 and 12. The banks encourage their employees to acquire professional qualifications and will often grant day-release and/or study leave.

Beyond the Clerical Grades

Each bank has its own management structure and job titles vary; in some banks there is an intermediate management level between the clerical and management grades. As an assistant manager you would be responsible for the smooth running of the branch, or will lead a unit within an operations centre. You will monitor training needs of your staff and, in a branch situation, you will also carry out the more complex customer interviews.

There are a number of other possibilities for someone who has reached this stage: you could find yourself transferred to a head office department for a period of specialised work, such as planning, organisation and methods or personnel management, or to a regional head office where you might be assessing loan applications submitted by branches within that region, working as a personnel assistant, a training officer, or as a regional marketing assistant. You might spend a period of months travelling around the country as a member of the bank's internal audit team, visiting branches and departments to monitor work standards and procedures.

Branch Management

In order to be selected for a branch manager's post you must perform well in a junior manager's post. The manager has overall responsibility for the efficient running of the branch, for its profitability, and for marketing the bank's services. He or she must exercise judgement in making loans to branch customers, and is accountable for the safe repayment of loans made at the branch. Managers must be able to mix easily with all sorts of people; a bank's customers can include first-time account holders, pensioners, university students, small business owners and chairmen of large organisations. Managers visit the premises of their business customers, and those customers look to their manager for advice on a wide range of financial matters.

In a branch the manager leads and motivates the branch team, ensures that the staff identify opportunities to sell the bank's services, and will be judged by the success of the branch in developing a profitable business. A first managerial post will probably be in a small branch and promotion will be to bigger branches with larger accounts or to regional offices

Case Study

Derek is the manager of a traditional branch of a high street bank, and his branch still carries out all banking operations under one roof, rather than passing work to a district processing centre.

I joined the bank from school with O levels, started at the bottom and worked my way through. My first job was at a very large branch, where I worked for six months; then I went to a smaller branch in the same town. I also did a spell on our relief team, which supplies cashiers to the whole district. I've worked in virtually every branch in this area at one time or another. I was made manager's assistant, helping with borrowing requests, after 13 years, and after 19 years I was an assistant manager. I got my first branch on my own in just under 21 years. This is my second branch.

This is a small seaside town, 2,000–3,000 inhabitants, and we have an awful lot of personal customers. There's the retail trade and the holiday industry as well, but very little manufacturing. Most of my customers come to see me because they want to borrow money or be granted an overdraft. I enjoy being able to lend money, but of course I do have to refuse now and again and it's much more difficult saying 'No' than saying 'Yes'. Your training does help, but it's not an easy thing to be trained for. We did role play and all that sort of thing in management training school, but it can't be realistic and it never covers all the different things that happen. People are very reluctant to accept a negative answer, whereas, if you say 'Yes' they're very pleased and are happy to leave straight away. One does tend to run out of ways to say 'No' to some people. In fact, though, I enjoy it all. I don't find any of it particularly difficult. It gets frustrating from time to time, but perhaps I'm fortunate in that I'm a fairly relaxed sort of person and I don't suffer sleepless nights over accounts that are going a bit suspect, so it doesn't create mental problems for me.

I get in just before 9 in the morning and see to the opening of the post and deal with what needs to be dealt with. I have an audio secretary; she's the secretary for the whole branch, not exclusively for me. Then my assistant will appear with what we call the refer list, which is a computer-produced list of all the accounts which are out of order, which he's been through, and we discuss the things he thinks I might deal with. And then interspersed with these activities are telephone calls and customer appointments. Customer appointments tend to come in great lumps or none at all, they never even themselves out. Of course, not all my customers come to see me; I feel it very important to get out to visit my business customers. I like to see them in their own surroundings because that gives me a much clearer picture of their business than I can ever obtain from a talk in my office. Once a week I review the overdraft arrangements that are up for expiry, basically to see what's got to happen next, whether they've got to be written to or telephoned or just cancelled. There are reports to make to my control, members of staff have a query and come in to talk to me and obviously there are many other odd bits and pieces to see to. Late in the afternoon one is battening down the hatches, signing the post and making sure everything is in order outside and, hopefully, one's not too late leaving. There are ten of us in the branch and the administrative side of things is done by my assistant.

Where will I go from here? Well, I think there will be at least two more changes of branch before they put me out to grass. In the past one had to move around a fair amount, but it's always been within the same region. The opportunity comes up and you're rather foolish if you refuse it, certainly when you're lower down the ladder. Opportunities don't come up all that often and if you don't take them you'll possibly have to wait another couple of years. The next obvious step, when the time comes, would be a move to a slightly larger branch within the county. I don't see myself at head office; I've made it clear to my local bosses that I'm not interested in specialised work, nor in branch work outside the region. I'd rather stay here than move to another area to obtain a better job. It remains interesting because there's always something new cropping up and people are lovely. I love dealing with people and that's basically what I'm doing all day, either staff or telephone calls or customers. It's part of my job to be the ambassador of the bank and if I see somebody at the counter I wander out and have a chat and it doesn't always have to be about business. Of course, it does get boring from time to time - every job does - but even if I stay here for another four or five years, which is not impossible, I certainly won't get fed up. I have no great ambition; I'd hate to be in charge of our regional office, that's not me at all, it would be too impersonal. I am more suited to being in a branch where I have personal contact with customers and which is small enough for me to know all the staff well; that's where my strength lies, rather than in the actual mechanics of banking *à la* book.

Specialist Work

Each year the banks select members of staff to work in the specialist divisions, which are usually located at regional centres or at head office. Most of those chosen are on a management training scheme, but occasionally there are direct entrants with GCSE or A levels (or equivalent) or a relevant degree.

Trust Divisions

A bank can act as executor of a will, either alone or jointly with a relative or close friend of the testator. It can handle personal tax returns, and will undertake the management of the investments of its customers, or look after investments until a beneficiary comes of age and is entitled to receive the capital from a will or settlement. Trust officers are expected to give advice on estate planning, particularly in connection with the avoidance of inheritance tax. The work is very specialised and demands a thorough working knowledge of relevant sections of current law.

International Division

A bank has to meet the needs of both small private customers and overseas trading operations of UK industry. This can involve providing such facilities as a speedy payments transfer system, dealing in foreign exchange, handling trade documents, financing imports and exports and advising on international trading conditions. It would be a mistake to imagine that working in the international division will lead to a posting abroad. Most of the staff are based in London or the regional branches of the division. The major clearing banks all have overseas branches but these are staffed mainly by local people. (See also Chapter 5, International Banking.)

Computer Centres

Computers play a crucial role in the organisation of a bank. Increasingly each work-station in a branch or department will have a terminal, and all members of staff are expected to enter data concerning customers with whom they have had contact, amending address or occupation details, recording applications for loan facilities, or detailing services which have been offered to their customers. All cheque and credit clearing and accounting is computerised; information on accounts is held on a main-frame computer, normally located at one or more centralised site.

At the main computer centres there are openings for trainee operators, programmers and systems analysts. Most of these staff are recruited from the locality in which the computer centres are situated. If you are interested in this type of work and you know that a major bank operates such a centre near to your home you should apply direct to that bank's computer centre (addresses on pp. 99 and 100).

Secretarial Work

Technology now offers word processing systems on the computer terminals intalled at each branch or office. These systems produce standard letters to customers for most routine services. However there are still openings for copy-typists, for audio and very occasionally shorthand secretaries: typically they will be located at a regional office or at a centre serving a number of branches within a locality, although some of the larger branches have retained secretaries under their roof. Applicants should have a good education, be able to write grammatically and spell correctly, a typing speed of 35–40 words per minute is expected. It is useful to have had audio training, and you should expect to work mainly with word processors. Although there are opportunities for promotion, secretarial jobs are non-career posts.

Other Specialist Work

Within the clearing banks are opportunities for many specialists. Some work is performed by people recruited directly into the specialisation, others transfer across functional boundaries. If for example your interest is in marketing, financial analysis, property management, corporate finance, stockbroking, investment management, strategic planning, or risk management, to list just a few jobs, then you may have a chance to work in one or more of these fields.

Opportunities and Prospects

Until fairly recently banking was a growth area with recruitment on the increase in many parts of the country, but since 1990, there has been a heavy reduction in staffing levels, and a selective programme of early retirement has taken place to adjust staff numbers to bank requirements. Throughout this period most banks have continued with a certain level of graduate recruitment; at the time of writing (1994) there are perhaps up to 1,000 graduates recruited each year, most of them regarded as potential management trainees. The remainder of localised recruitment needs have often been satisfied by fixed-term contracts. These may continue for some years but staff who feel secure and confident of career progression will perform better, and will offer a higher standard of service to customers. The banks also recognise the need to motivate their staff and there are signs of fixed-term employees being offered permanent staff contracts. At the time of writing in late 1994 there are more positive signs for general recruitment throughout the banking industry than has been the case for several years.

The banks look after their employees well and encourage them to realise their potential. Promotion is on merit, not length of service and, for the most able, management level is often attained in your twenties. You must be prepared to move between branches, although generally within a geographical region. Refusing the offer of a posting can mean that your promotion chances are restricted.

Several banks operate a re-entry and reservist scheme, which allows able career bankers (women or men) to take up to five years off work, for example to raise their children, or to care for dependent relatives, returning to a post at the same level as the one they occupied before leaving. While away they are sent information which will keep them abreast of new developments and they are asked to do a minimum of two weeks' paid relief work per year.

Annual Starting Salaries

Salaries vary from bank to bank and if you want to know exactly what each one pays you must consult the careers literature. The following (1994) figures, provided by the Banking Information Service, tell you approximately what you can expect.

School-/college-leavers	£6,200–£9,800
Graduates	£12,700–£14,800

London Allowance

Extra allowances are paid to staff employed within the following distances from Charing Cross. Most banks pay at, or close to, the following scale:

0– 6 miles	£3,600
6–10 miles	£2,450
10–16 miles	£2,250
16–22 miles	£1,400

An allowance of £750 pa is available to staff working in certain branches in South East England and £298 pa to staff employed in certain other large towns.

Most banks operate a profit-sharing scheme and pay an annual percentage bonus at the end of each year.

Chapter 3

Girobank

Introduction

Girobank was launched in 1968 as a convenient and rapid money transmission service operated by the Post Office. In 1983 it was granted clearing bank status and is now a subsidiary of the Alliance & Leicester Building Society, serving two million business and personal customers.[1] It is different enough from the other clearing banks to merit a chapter to itself.

Girobank's services to personal customers include the maintenance of current and deposit accounts, credit and cash card facilities, payment of standing orders, issuing travellers' cheques and foreign currency, revolving credit facilities and insurance. Its corporate services include current account banking, rent collection, a service for depositing business takings, a change-giving service, money market deposits, and international money transmission payment and collection services.

Operating Structure

In total, Girobank employs 4,000 people, the majority working in the administrative and operational centre at Bootle (Merseyside). Here the bulk of the transactions are processed using advanced computer technology. The head office, which deals with all aspects of the domestic and foreign banking and money markets, is in London, and customer accounts are cared for from a network of regional offices (Liverpool, Birmingham, Leeds and Ashford). There are nine regional corporate service offices and cheque remittance centres in Northern Ireland, Scotland and London.

[1] Since this chapter was written, Girobank's personal banking operations have been transferred to the parent company; Girobank now carries out only the corporate banking services which are based mainly at Bootle.

Girobank's cashiering services and other face-to-face transactions with customers are performed by Post Office counter clerks, who are not Girobank employees. Telecare, the bank's premier phone and mail banking service, also enables customers to discuss account-related matters from the comfort of their home or offices on weekdays from 8.30am to 8.30pm and until 1pm on Saturdays. Telecare receives more than 100,000 customer calls each week.

The Clerical Grades

The Work

As Girobank is a large organisation, the duties of those in clerical grades can vary considerably according to the needs of each department. However, as a general overview, responsibilities can cover areas such as office administration, opening and managing customer accounts, sales, and public relations work.

There are currently four clerical grades, numbered 1 to 4, of which the latter is the most senior position. In addition the Bank employs Data Processing Officers (DPOs), responsible for the processing and preparation of information through computers. From DPO you can gain promotion to the higher grade of Senior Data Processing Officer.

Training

When you join Girobank you will be given on-the-job training backed up with in-house courses. Your future training needs will be considered in the light of your job performance requirements, your potential and your personal aspirations. Your performance will be formally assessed once a year and you will have the opportunity to discuss and plan your career development with your immediate manager. Where necessary, Girobank will provide financial assistance for you to pursue external technical or academic training.

Entry Requirements

Most school-leavers join Girobank at Clerical Grade 1. It is desirable to have two GCSEs (or equivalent) including English language, but if you have no academic qualifications you can still apply and you will be asked to take a test at the time of your interview. If you apply for a Clerical Grade 4 post you will need a minimum of five GCSEs (or equivalent), one of which must be

English language, and it will be an advantage to have passes at Grade C or above.

In 1995, Girobank was not seeking to employ people for clerical grades. However, candidates register interest by requesting an application form from the Bank.

Management Trainees

Each year Girobank recruits a number of management trainees, consisting of graduates holding a degree in an appropriate discipline, and young managers who have already established their career in a relevant field within the Bank. The management training programme lasts for two years and is designed to enhance potential by increasing professional and managerial skills. Girobank also recruits a number of commercial placement students each year; they are students on a sandwich degree course (or equivalent) interested in pursuing a career with the bank after graduating, and meanwhile wishing to broaden their management experience. The Commercial Placement Programme is similar to the Management Training Programme, but is of just 48 weeks duration.

The Work

Management Trainees and Commercial Placement Students can choose to work within one of the following areas of the Bank:

- ☐ Corporate and Personal Banking: acting as interface between Girobank and its customers.
- ☐ Finance: providing a contribution to the financial planning and controlling of the Bank's main activities.
- ☐ Audit and Investigation: assisting in the development of cost-effective controls within the Bank.
- ☐ Operations: helping to improve the Bank's efficiency through work-flow control, statistical analysis, resourcing and organisational planning.
- ☐ Information Technology: involvement with investment in computer technology which is essential to the Bank's growth and success.
- ☐ Personnel & Training: helping to ensure the Bank's inner resources meet business needs.

Training

Every management trainee receives an individual 'tailor-made' development programme which includes practical experience within their chosen specialist area, project work and Bank internal or external courses to support development. Trainees are encouraged (through financial support and study leave) to acquire professional qualifications which may be in a management, banking, accounting, or personnel and training field.

Which Degree?

Girobank recruits graduates who have a degree in an 'appropriate' discipline; recruitment literature mentions business studies, banking, economics or statistics, marketing, civil engineering, law, mathematics, computer studies, industrial relations and commercially oriented or quantitative disciplines.

Personal Characteristics

The selection process is based on a combination of interviews and tests which identify a candidate's potential, ability and interests. Girobank looks for highly motivated individuals who have confidence, strong interpersonal skills and an ability to work under pressure whilst making a positive contribution to the success of the business.

Vacancies

Vacancies are advertised in the national press and through university careers services. Enquiries should be addressed to the Recruitment Co-ordinator based in Girobank's Personnel Unit, Bootle (address on p. 101).

Annual Starting Salaries (1994)

Starting salaries are flexible depending on levels of skill and expertise. Current salary scales are as follows:

Grade	*Minimum*	*Maximum*
Clerical Grade 1	£ 5,785	£ 8,901
Clerical Grade 2	£ 6,523	£11,239
Clerical Grade 3	£ 7,177	£14,751
Clerical Grade 4	£12,790	£16,464

In addition, a territorial allowance of £3,500 is paid to staff working in the London area.

Chapter 4

Credit Card Companies

Introduction

The two main credit card payment systems in the UK are VISA and MasterCard. The country's largest card issuing company, Barclaycard, offers credit cards under both brand names, as do most of the other major issuers. Just as the international brand, VISA, is now widely recognised within the UK, so is MasterCard now identified alongside the UK brand, Access, and the continental Eurocard. A large number of banks, building societies and financial institutions are now able to offer cards bearing either logo.

A more recent development is the growth of debit payment cards under the Switch and Delta badges, which are linked to the bank or building society account balances maintained by the card-holder with the card issuing company.

The banks, building societies, etc., all have card issuing divisions; they recruit their own cardholders and finance the balances outstanding on their cardholders' accounts. Not all of the card issuers provide card processing services. Barclaycard performs this service for its own cards, and for other card issuers, as does Bank of Scotland. TSB Bank (Trustcard) processes its own cards. Another specialist card processor acting for a number of major issuers is First Data Resources. These companies provide facilities for card issuing companies who have chosen not to carry out this function for themselves. They undertake transaction services including authorisation, data entry, statement issue, etc. and obtain their revenue from tariffs for the services provided to their clients, the card issuing companies, and to the merchants (such as retailers) whose card vouchers they process.

The Work

Most of the work in this area is concerned with data processing. A growing proportion of transactions and authorisations are handled electronically, and each week the companies process several million sales vouchers and handle enquiries from retailers requesting authorisation for transactions. This work is done by VDU operators, who need a pleasant telephone manner and an aptitude for keyboard work. Computer operators' duties include printing large volumes of statements, and there is work for computer programmers and systems analysts.

You can expect a basic 35-hour week, but shift and bank holiday work will be a feature.

Entry Requirements

After several years of minimal activity, general recruitment has been resumed. The main intake is of school-leavers with GCSEs (or equivalent) who become trainee VDU operators or trainee computer operators. Trainee computer programmers, systems analysts or systems programmers need A levels (or equivalent). There is a small intake of graduates, some of whom will have specialist computer skills. You should apply for a post during your final year at school or college.

Training

The training, most of which is given on the job, is backed up with in-house courses. Training for computer programmers, systems analysts or systems programmers is likely to last for a minimum of two months. There is a management training scheme, and graduate entrants will gain experience of operations, risk management, marketing, and financial control, as well as information technology, before selection for general management opportunities, or a career in one of the specialist functions.

Addresses are on p. 101.

Chapter 5

International Banking

Introduction

In the 1980s world trade expanded rapidly and there was a corresponding expansion in the range of services offered by banks; nearly all now have an international division and associated companies operating in most of the world's major financial centres. International banks have customers throughout the world and on their behalf deal in the foreign exchange currency markets and in international stock and bond investments, handle foreign trade documents, offer banking accounts and loans in all major international trading currencies, and provide advice on overseas trading opportunities to their UK-based commercial customers. They will arrange specialised loans or finance for international trading contracts. All the high street banks have international divisions and many have subsidiary companies in major overseas trading centres. All will have a network of agents, or 'correspondent banks' who will act on their behalf, and on behalf of the clearing bank's customers in locations where the UK bank has no local branch network.

There are also large specialist international banks like Standard Chartered Bank, and The Hongkong and Shanghai Banking Corporation (HSBC) which now owns Midland Bank. Some 400 foreign banks have offices in London.

International Work with the High Street Banks

In Chapter 2, international banking was mentioned in the context of the high street banks. Each has an international division which provides a comprehensive overseas banking service for its UK customers, and acts as correspondent bank, or agent, in the UK for banks abroad. Many UK banks maintain branches abroad and others operate through agency arrangements with foreign banks.

The international divisions of almost all the high street banks have their headquarters in London. Most have branches or specialist foreign trade centres in major provincial cities, and many have branches in a number of foreign capitals and cities. Opportunities for British staff to work abroad are, however, limited as most members of staff are recruited from the country in which the branch is situated. Generally only relatively few staff are sent abroad on secondment; they will have been identified as having excellent management potential and will be expected to be fluent in more than one language.

Our membership of the European Union has changed the employment market within this country. Applicants will be in competition with students from elsewhere in Europe: those from France or Germany, for example, are often fluent in at least one other language. Already major banks are recruiting graduates from European universities. It is not essential to have a language degree, but fluency in a second or third language will enhance your attraction to a prospective employer.

Entry Requirements

Most bank employees started work at the age of 18 when they left school or college. Since the early 1990s most clearing banks have restricted their non-graduate recruitment to short-term contracts of one or two years. However, there are signs that some of those contract staff may be offered permanent staff status when their contracts are due for renewal.

Banks differ in the academic qualifications they ask for; most will expect their staff to be educated to GCSE (or equivalent) standard, including English and mathematics. There are opportunities for A-level applicants, and all major banks have maintained their programme of graduate selection and recruitment: this is a highly competitive process, and for those who meet the criteria, the programme may include attendance at an assessment centre where you will be put in a number of situations to assess your skills and competences. You will be encouraged to undertake some research about the organisation before submitting your application.

Training

The international divisions of the clearing banks, and the London offices of foreign banks, have training programmes similar to those of the high street banks. For those entering clerical posts most of the training will be on the job. For graduates, and for some A-level entrants considered to have management potential, there is an intensive training programme introducing you to most aspects of international banking. The programme may include an overseas assignment of a few months to aid familiarisation with the bank's international culture. For those remaining on the management training programme there will be a programme of continuing development: emphasis is placed on obtaining appropriate professional qualifications, and graduates may be encouraged to follow an MBA course.

The Work

Much of the work, which can involve dealing in very large sums of money, has to be executed at speed and carries a high stress rating. Great accuracy is called for at all times. The foreign exchange market is open 24 hours a day, so certain dealers will work an early or a late shift, or on some public holidays.

Telex and terminal operation. People with basic typing skills are recruited for this work. Telex operators send information to banks abroad. Terminal operators input information into the computerised accounting system which enables international money transfers to be made.

Cables. International banks use sophisticated communication systems and have sections dealing with the transmission of money transfers and messages by cable, telex and SWIFT (Society for Worldwide Interbank Financial Telecommunication).

Payments. Payments clerks handle payments from all over the world in all currencies. Many of these transactions are urgent and involve very large sums of money.

Documentary credits. This department handles documents relating to imports and exports, and its work involves opening, amending and paying letters of credit. As payments must be made in strict accordance with the terms of the letters of credit, the work demands close attention to detail.

Exchange dealing. Foreign exchange dealers facilitate the buying and selling of large amounts of currency for international trading transactions. Those entering this complex area of dealing need a working knowledge of the accounting side of foreign exchange. Most importantly, they need to have a flair for dealing, a trader's instinct, and to have a sharp mind and quick reactions. Foreign exchange dealing is one of the most demanding areas of international banking, but can be one of the most rewarding.

Other work could include the issuing to branches of foreign notes and travellers' cheques, arranging loans for multi-national corporations or for overseas governments, buying and selling foreign bonds and securities, or marketing the bank's services in the international marketplace.

Career Structure

The career structure is similar to that in branch banking with clerical, junior management and managerial grades. For staff of the international division of the clearing banks, or London-based staff of the foreign banks, salaries and benefits are broadly comparable with those of the high street banks (see p. 40). However, the graduate recruitment policies of leading international banks will, typically, incorporate an aim to be among the upper quartile of graduate salaries in each country in which they operate.

Once you have worked your way through the clerical grades (the speed at which you do this will depend on your qualifications at entry and performance on the job), you reach junior management (and in some banks have the title 'appointed officer'). At this level you could work as a staff supervisor, systems officer responsible for communication plans, branch accountant or manager's assistant.

Promotion to management depends on experience and performance. Managerial posts are both varied and challenging. You could join the management team of a provincial foreign business centre, in which case your responsibilities may include the work of the unit, and liaising with branches of the bank in your catchment area, promoting good relations with their customers involved in international trading. Most overseas secondments are at management level, and the importance of language skills cannot be over-emphasised.

Further information in international work with the clearing banks is available from the personnel departments of their head offices, or from the international banks themselves (see addresses on p. 101).

Foreign Banks

Just as British banks represent the UK (and some foreign companies) overseas, so many foreign banks have branches in Britain. At the last count, 400 overseas banks have branches in London, some also with offices in major provincial cities. These banks originally came to represent customers from their countries of origin. Now many of them fulfil a much wider role: they compete with UK clearing banks for the business of larger companies, they offer investment banking services alongside British merchant banks, and some have made strategic investments in specialised finance houses or equipment-leasing businesses.

The larger foreign banks are active in the graduate recruitment market, competing with major UK employers. Starting salaries tend to be at the upper end of the ranges quoted on page 40. Most, but not always all, of the top London jobs tend to go to employees from the banks' countries of origin, and so you should weigh long-term opportunities against short-term benefits when considering applications to this sector. The list on pp. 102–6 includes all foreign banks identified as having 100 or more employees in 1994, but there are many organisations with staff numbers just below this level which may offer comparable opportunities, and so further research is encouraged.

Chapter 6

Merchant Banks

Introduction

It is difficult to provide clear and precise information about merchant banks for two reasons: first, there is no such thing as a typical merchant bank, and second, this is a business whose activities change with the markets, and with the demands of clients. In essence the job of a merchant banker is to provide or find whatever financial service the customer requires.

The term 'merchant bank' was originally applied to business houses which changed from trading in their own right to financing the commercial activities of others, particularly abroad. However, the term now increasingly used is 'investment bank', reflecting the radical changes which began in the mid-1980s. At that time the whole system and organisation of the Stock Exchange was deregulated; many of the rules and practices were abolished in what became known as 'Big Bang' in 1986. This permitted companies, particularly banks and merchant banks, to participate directly in stockbroking and making markets in shares; their large capital resources enabled them to trade on a wider basis and to expand their dealing in international securities, reinforcing London's position as a leading international financial centre.

The distinction between domestic business and foreign business has virtually disappeared and the globalisation of merchant banking business has led to more activity being denominated in other currencies than is now conducted in sterling. Just how banks have organised themselves for this globalisation of their activity has varied from bank to bank: some have opened their own offices in New York, Tokyo, Seoul, or wherever; others have formed partnerships with local firms, while yet others have bought shareholdings in appropriate entities. But as a result of these changes, few of London's merchant banks now have more business within the UK than in the rest of the world.

The factor which made these changes possible was information technology. Instant communications, computerised databases, and large-scale computing power enabled markets to be linked across the world, new complex financial instruments to be developed, and new financial opportunities to open up for large corporations. This gave merchant banks a choice of strategy: either they could expand to become a broadly based international securities firm, or they could remain small but specialise in particular niches in the increasingly complex world of finance.

Compared with the high street banks, merchant banks are small - the largest ones employing 3,000 to 4,000 people, the smallest fewer than 100. The majority of people in merchant banking work in the City of London; there are some provincial offices, and selected staff are seconded to work overseas for periods, typically of two to five years. Now about half the merchant banks in London are foreign-owned.

The Work

A merchant bank will advise a company wishing to expand on the best way to raise money; this might be by issuing more shares, borrowing, or by a stock market flotation. In order to get flotation business a bank needs not only an impeccable reputation but expert and committed staff. A merchant bank's mergers and acquisitions team may be called upon to advise a company which has identified a firm it would like to take over, or to look for a suitable firm for its clients to take over. But not all changes of ownership are adversarial; the bank will act in non-hostile deals such as management buy-outs, or demergers. It will suggest ways of financing the takeover, and help to conduct negotiations and prepare documents - the most important of which would be the offer document.

Merchant banks also give their clients general financial advice; they keep a company in touch with its investors, oversee its relations with its main bankers, make sure that it is getting the best possible financing arrangements and liaise with the press. Investment management is an extremely important business for many merchant banks, and London has a high reputation for its expertise in this area. Other activities include: bullion dealing, treasury services, securities dealing, and the provision of venture and development capital. Many have developed high levels of professionalism in derivatives: these are products created to allow investors to benefit from the rises and falls in, for example, currencies, interest rates, or share indices, and which are used mainly by institutional investors to help them to manage their risk of exposure to sudden movements in those markets.

The traditional image of the merchant banker - male, middle-aged, pin-stripe suited, clinching huge deals over brandy and cigars in panelled rooms - dies hard, but nothing could be further from the reality. Nowadays, a woman is as likely as a man to be recruited. The average age in a division could be as low as 30; the work is not all conducted round a table; wellington boots and a hard hat replace city clothes when visits to building sites are called for; the oak panelling has generally been ripped out to make way for banks of VDUs in open-plan offices; and in many banks not even the cigar smoke remains; indeed, in most office buildings smoking is forbidden.

Recruitment

Although most houses recruit at a number of different levels, opportunities for those without at least A levels are limited nowadays.

Entry Requirements

A Levels (or equivalent)

There is a small intake of recruits with A levels (or equivalent) or a business studies diploma. Such people begin in a clerical post. Promotion prospects depend on performance and there are excellent opportunities for advancement.

Graduate Entrants

Which Degree?

Most houses require the degree to be at least a 2.1 and, while few banks state a preference for a specific discipline, some would deem the most useful subjects to be economics, law or business studies. Graduates may be recruited to fill specific posts, in which case they would start work very early on and receive on-the-job training, or they may go into a pool and be placed after an initial training period.

Personal Qualities

In all applicants, interviewers are looking for evidence of motivation, maturity and self-confidence. Graduates are given responsibility early in their careers and must, therefore, be equal to tough negotiating, high-level client contact, and contact with other professionals such as lawyers and accountants. Some branches of the work, eg corporate finance, generate a lot of paperwork and call for the ability to grasp essentials and get the details right. Imagination, diligence and flexibility are important qualities in any candidate, and fluency in foreign languages is an asset. There is often a high stress factor to cope with as much of the work involves huge sums of money and has to be done to strict deadlines. The rewards are substantial for those who perform well, but to earn those rewards you could find yourself working 12-hour days and six-day weeks in a tough, competitive atmosphere.

Training and Professional Qualifications

Most technical training for clerical work is given on the job, unless specific training needs are highlighted by the annual performance appraisal.

No degree, however seemingly 'relevant', equips you to start work straight away and, of course, if your degree subject is totally unrelated to banking, you have everything to learn. All graduates will receive some sort of induction; whether this lasts a matter of days, weeks or months will depend on the individual bank's training policy. You could spend your first few months working your way round the different departments of the bank, being trained on the job and breaking off to attend courses on such topics as finance or investment management; or you could be plunged into a period of intense training consisting of lectures, seminars, case work and outside visits. Whatever your bank's training policy, you are likely to be trained by both in-house staff and professionals from outside. Before management trainees are allowed, or expected, to take part in making deals, they have to get to grips with the routine aspects of the business.

All staff are encouraged to obtain an appropriate professional qualification. This will often be a Master's degree in Business Administration (MBA), or a legal or accountancy qualification. Generally, study leave is granted and payment made to cover tuition costs, examination fees and the cost of textbooks.

It is not uncommon for merchant banks who wish to fill a specific vacancy to recruit those with an appropriate professional qualification or relevant experience obtained with another employer. Such people may be offered a permanent post or a contract for a specified period; they enter at a higher level than graduate trainees and have less groundwork to cover. The larger merchant banks are among the leading users of information technology. There is a steady demand for applicants with high-level IT skills and experience.

Salaries

Salaries vary from employer to employer. Those for clerical workers will probably be comparable with the salaries paid by the high street banks (see p. 40).

In management grades, salaries are commensurate with performance, and performance is not simply a crude calculation of how much money you have generated in your business dealing; it could, for example, be your contribution to the organisation of your department, or your participation in such activities as recruiting or company presentations. A basic starting salary for graduate trainees is likely to be between £18,000 and £25,000. You could be earning £50,000 by the time you reach your mid-thirties and, in addition, be eligible for a bonus, a subsidised mortgage, free life and medical insurance and a company car. High flyers can earn considerably more.

Case Studies

Lindsey obtained a Master's degree in finance at Strathclyde, and now works in Kleinwort Benson's Treasury Division.[1]

> The Treasury Division manages the bank's money assets as well as those of its clients, corporations, institutions and private individuals. Core trading activities involve dealing in the money markets to raise loans and invest capital, and trading in foreign exchange, international bonds, gilt-edged stock, corporate loans and derivatives.
>
> We take advantage of variations in interest and currency rates to generate income and manage the risk our clients face as rates change.

[1] These case studies are reproduced, with permission, from Kleinwort Benson's graduate recruitment brochure. Kleinwort Benson is now owned by Germany's Dresdner Bank, and employs some 4,000 people worldwide. Although similar career opportunities to those described in these case studies may be found in other merchant banks, it should be emphasised that no two such institutions are alike.

This involves developing and trading in sophisticated products such as options, swaps and other derivatives - and running our own managed investment funds. All these are fast-moving and highly competitive markets so we're constantly developing new products to stay in the forefront.

Treasury offers opportunities for graduates in trading, sales and research. My joining the Derivatives Product Group coincided with the launch of one of the first investment trusts to invest in Over-the-Counter Derivatives. I became involved immediately - preparing reports and managing currency risk. My involvement in the integral trading of the small, tightly managed, hands-on team followed quickly.

Very soon I had to take my own position in the market. This forced me to focus and make decisions in a way no amount of prior analysis could ever do. Recently, I was given the opportunity to monitor our positions in all the European books with a view to trading and managing in the near future.

The nature of trading is such that you cannot be assigned tasks. Training takes the form of guidance as to what sort of trades may be successful rather than learning specific rules which define what amounts to a good trade. Discovery of those profit-making trades is a constant challenge which ambitious people thrive upon. The work is self-motivated, and for those who are, reward can come quickly - my manager was a graduate three years ago.

What do you need to do well in Treasury? Judgement and the ability to learn as you work. Analysis is important, but it's not enough on its own. We look at economic fundamentals - but the market hasn't followed the textbooks since I joined! We're all looking at the same screens for something in those prices that makes a good trade - and seeing opportunities depends on inspiration and innovation. You can't really be taught: you learn by doing it. You also need a responsible attitude and attention to detail: you will have the power to put the bank's name - and its money - on the line . . . You need to be determined: you'll be under pressure, and disappointments are inevitable when the markets turn against you . . . And you need to be alert and persuasive, to sell your ideas to other people, especially if you're trading.

Vittorio obtained a degree in European Business Administration at the European Business School. He now works in Kleinwort Benson's Financing and Advisory Division.

The division has two broad areas of activity: corporate advisory, and financing. The corporate finance team advises many companies, both in the UK and overseas, including major international groups. The advice covers all forms of equity and equity-related finance, for example flotations (a private company selling shares to the public for the first time), privatisations, and finance for acquisitions or other major projects. The team also helps clients to find acquisition targets, to make and defend against takeover bids, and to buy and sell private businesses.

The financing sector of the division arranges public and private debt finance for companies and projects. Assignments range from a simple leasing package for a company car fleet, to highly sophisticated structures funding long-term infrastructure projects such as dams and airports. Variations in interest and exchange rates, movements in bond markets and differences in national tax and accounting regimes all provide opportunities to develop ingenious products and structures that benefit our clients.

In international corporate finance you're quickly given a lot of responsibility for results. It pays to think laterally. When a director asked me to research information superhighways, I remembered it was a subject that was high on President Clinton's agenda. I phoned the White House, and managed to find out that the president's top adviser on the subject was visiting London. I called his hotel, miraculously found him in his room, and persuaded him to see me. Fifteen minutes later I was on my way to a private meeting with him. His hosts - a firm we know well - arrived for *their* briefing as I left. I think they were quite impressed.

The key difference between a good corporate financier and a mediocre one, is the planning and organising. You're working on different deals with different timetables and different degrees of urgency - you must organise yourself well and delegate, upwards as well as downwards. You need energy and stamina too: the equities and treasury people start work earlier than we do, but we regularly work well into the evening. Integrity and good judgement are essential - so is financial analytical ability. You need the job motivation to work on your own initiative and strong ability in written communications; your reports will have to convince the people who run major companies. The great satisfaction of the job is the chance to meet and influence these people - and your success will be recognised.

Kathryn joined Kleinwort Benson Securities in 1992 after reading history at Oxford University.

Our equities division, KBS, is a leading London institutional broker. It researches and deals in the shares of UK, European, Hong Kong, Japanese and emerging market companies, and raises money for companies on stock exchanges around the world. It is also a corporate broker acting for many UK clients. The corporate broking team plays a vital role in the flotation of companies and in ensuring that the corporate clients are close to their institutional shareholders. With particular emphasis on market-related aspects, it also provides advice on fund-raising and on takeovers and mergers.

I joined the equities research team where we analyse companies' performance and prospects. I chose this work because you get an early opportunity to talk to companies direct, and to write and present your own views. There is never an average day in equities. If a company's price starts moving suddenly you have to stand up and get the attention of the dealing room and argue the case for what you think is going to happen. You've got to convince the sales force - who have their own expertise and are going to have to convince their own clients.

Much of what happens in the market depends on sentiment and speculation, so although analysis is valuable, you have to add your own judgement. It's all about getting people to trust you and to deal on the basis of what you recommend. Some banks may not recognise the benefit of broad experience between departments, but here you have contacts all over the bank, from the training programme onwards. You need energy, determination and skills in written communications and oral presentation, because you are competing with other research teams for the sales team's attention. It's all very public, so you must enjoy being accountable for what you've achieved. The satisfaction comes from discovering that you're becoming a real expert whose ideas carry weight - while knowing that the learning never stops. They teach you how to swim - then they show you the deep end!

Richard read Politics, Philosophy and Economics at Oxford, and now works with Kleinwort Benson Investment Management.

The investment management division creates wealth for institutional and private clients worldwide. Success is achieved by providing innovative and responsive investment and banking services.

Our institutional asset management business invests to give clients the best possible return, usually dealing within agreed policies. We provide portfolio management services for charities, insurance companies, investment trusts, mutual and pensions funds and in some cases for companies themselves. We invest in shares, money market instruments, bonds and currencies and operate our own managed funds.

You work from day one here, so you've got to be good at learning on the job and picking it up as you go. For example, macroeconomics is crucial, but you won't get a real grasp from a book - the best training you get is sitting with the rest of the team and listening to them talk. You're constantly writing reports to clients and other parts of the bank. You're also reporting in person, so you need to have strong interpersonal skills, and to be able to put forward your case fluently. Someone who has done dozens of presentations since joining

Kleinwort Benson told me the most important thing is to get enthusiastic about every single one. It helps if you're an extrovert - an analytical extrovert with sound judgement, if that's not asking too much!

I've been pleasantly surprised by the amount of people-work involved, and you meet some very influential people. I'm now managing a US-based investment trust, reporting monthly to the board in writing, and six-monthly in person in New York. They're a very challenging group, who have drawn on all the skills I've learned: one is a diplomat who helped make all the politics we're talking about, another is a former US treasury secretary who helped make the economics I'm reporting on. These people shaped the subjects I studied, and now they're saying: 'So, Richard, what do *you* think . . . ?

Richard's colleague Sarupa read Spanish and European Studies at Warwick. She is a portfolio manager in KBIM Private Bank.

Our private bank provides banking and portfolio management for individuals, with services including mortgages and loans, financial planning, inheritance and tax planning on an international basis. Clients consult me about their wealth the same way they see a doctor about their health.

We start the day with a meeting at 8.45 to keep us up-to-date on investment policy, market announcements and the kind of transactions we may need to make. But after that, you handle anything your clients throw at you. You listen, you advise, and in between you're constantly looking for opportunities to improve their financial wellbeing.

Our business is about relationships, trust and integrity. Getting on with people is the number one requirement. But judgement, responsibility, and attention to detail are also crucial, because we have a very direct kind of responsibility: we're directly answerable to individuals for managing their money, and sometimes their livelihoods.

We are given broad guidelines for investments, but within those you make your own decisions based on clients' individual needs. You need to be resourceful - not all information is readily at your fingertips but there's enough knowledge within the team to ensure that no question goes unanswered. Written and oral communication is also a big part of our job - your time is divided between communicating with clients and with portfolio management. And you have to be a good listener, hearing what people mean, not just what they say.

Chapter 7
Finance Houses

Introduction

Finance houses lend to consumers and all types of businesses. Many are owned by banks, others by retailers, building societies, manufacturers or insurance companies; some are independent. The first finance houses were formed in the nineteenth century to finance railway wagons for the coal industry and to provide hire purchase for sewing machines. The mass production of the motor car gave a great impetus to the industry. Now over five million individuals and hundreds of thousands of businesses are customers of finance houses.

Finance houses provide credit for the purchase of cars (the largest single category), houses, home improvements and all kinds of consumer durables. Types of finance available include personal loans where no security is given and repayment is over a fixed period. When larger sums are involved, finance houses may require security by way of a first or second mortgage. Cars are frequently financed on hire purchase where the customers agree to hire the goods for an agreed period, paying by instalments. A relatively new product in the car market is the personal contract purchase. Finance houses also issue credit cards and store cards. Much of the credit offered by finance houses is at the point of sale, ie in the high street store, or through major dealers.

Finance houses enable businesses to acquire equipment of every sort, from small office items to aircraft and ships. They provide leasing facilities - both finance leases and operating leases, including contract hire; hire purchase; conditional sale; stocking finance; block discounting and a variety of business loans.

Although lending rose steadily throughout the 1980s, the economic climate brought about a drop in new lending in 1990,

1991 and 1992. In 1993 the market recovered with an increase in new lending of 17 per cent, although consumer credit performed better than business finance.

Structure

A medium-sized to large finance house will employ people in sales, marketing, IT, finance, personnel and administration roles. Furthermore, skills in the use of desk-top computers and software, and an ability to develop high standards in customer relationships and in customer service are actively sought.

Recruitment, Entry Requirements and Training

Entry-level jobs may be advertised in the local press and Jobcentres. Vacancies for experienced, professionally qualified staff, or for graduates, generally appear in the national press.

Finance houses may recruit school leavers with GCSEs (or equivalent), preferably in English and mathematics at Grade 'C' or above. Naturally, entry-level jobs are an introduction to the business of credit finance and cover a variety of functions. Good communication skills and an ability to use the telephone in a business-like manner are important, as are numeracy and a good command of the English language.

A-level entrants would generally expect to see career expectations initially accelerated but, as for all staff, there would be encouragement to acquire professional qualifications in one's chosen career as a basic building block. Thereafter continuing study to broaden one's knowledge would also be encouraged.

Across the leasing industry many finance houses actively seek graduate recruits, both fresh from university with a career to build, and others with established commercial skills. In particular, employers may focus on IT, accountancy, and corporate sales, with a relevant qualification in one of these disciplines as an objective.

Training has a key role to play in jobs at all levels in a finance house, to reinforce the culture of quality in a highly competitive industry.

The Work

With the development of telephone-based financial services in the retail sector, and to some extent in the corporate sector, a career in sales offers a prime opportunity for those who seek a challenging and rewarding start to their careers. In addition, there is always a demand for individuals with strong interpersonal skills and an instinct for the 'cut and thrust' of negotiating with clients to conclude a deal which benefits both parties.

Pre-eminently, the sales force is a finance house's front line, and individuals with tenacity, personality, patience, and who can form sound business relationships, are highly valued members of the team.

You will discover that finance houses demand from employees a high standard of service to their clients. It is important that the impression which you create reflects these standards so that the client is happy to carry out further business with your company. However, some clients fall into financial difficulty, and staff engaged in the collection of outstanding debt will need to exercise skills that range from tact and diplomacy to firmness in negotiation. Management would be expected to take direct responsibility for the more protracted and difficult cases.

Finance houses obtain business from a variety of sources. These include direct sales to clients as a result of advertising, links with vehicle manufacturers, and introductions from brokers who act as middle men between the client and the finance house. To ensure that fresh business continues to be generated there are opportunities in marketing, which will include developing imaginative campaigns in liaison with the professional advertising agencies.

Everyone employed within this industry, whether in sales or in an administration role, can expect to work with a keyboard and VDU.

Remuneration

In general, finance houses review basic salaries on an annual basis according to an individual's assessed performance. In certain roles, usually sales related, incentive bonuses are paid in addition to basic salary, where sales targets have been fully met or exceeded. The larger finance houses also offer a range of benefits for staff including subsidised finance, and overall they are comparable with those of the major banks and building societies.

Case Study

Helen read pure mathematics at the Royal Holloway and Bedford

New College. Two years after joining her employers she is a member of the credit policy unit in one of the largest finance houses.

> On completion of my degree course I joined Barclays Mercantile Business Finance. In view of my degree in mathematics, I was immediately assigned to the risk team within one of the businesses forming BMBF. After an initial training period I found myself having to consider deals coming forward from the field force, and determining whether they met the credit assessment policy, always bearing in mind there were some important customer relations at stake.
>
> After the first 12 months I was moved to the credit policy unit. As it was important that I understood the full breadth and range of the business, I had a number of attachments over several weeks to different functions within the company.
>
> Because I have a good level of skill in analysing and interpreting the data put before me, already I feel that I am making a worthwhile contribution to the long-term success of the business. Whilst all jobs require new employees to go through a period of training, I feel that it is important that an individual's skills are matched to a particular role in the business as soon as possible. Certainly, this is what my current company has done, giving me the opportunity to learn and to show that I can make a worthwhile contribution.
>
> I realise that it is important to continue to study so I'm currently involved with the Finance & Leasing Association's diploma which is already showing me how much there is to learn about the leasing and HP business.
>
> Ever since I was at university I had taken the view that I wanted to be associated with the finance industry, and ideally with the risk assessment part of that business. The good news is that I am actually applying what I learnt on my degree course to a real live situation whilst continuing to learn more and more as the days go by.

Information about the Finance & Leasing Association and the professional examinations is given in Chapter 13; the Association (address on p. 101) will supply a list of the names and addresses of its members.

Chapter 8

Department for National Savings

Introduction

The main aims of the Department for National Savings are: to attract personal savings as required by the Government's funding policy; to encourage the savings habit among a wide range of people; to market a range of products with particular emphasis on longer-term saving; and to give its customers a reliable, prompt and friendly service.

The Department, which employed 5,730 permanent staff at 1 April 1994, is split into three operational divisions and has a small London headquarters with a staff of 250. National Savings at Glasgow employs some 2,110 people. It provides investment and ordinary banking account facilities, Children's Bonus Bonds, First Option Bonds and Capital Bonds. The National Savings Certificates, Yearly Plan and Save As You Earn schemes are administered in Durham, where there is a staff of some 1,400. Pensioners Guaranteed Income Bonds, Income Bonds, the National Savings Stock Register and Premium Bonds are administered in the St Annes-Blackpool area where some 1,390 people are employed. A further 580 people are employed across all four locations on Information Systems support.

The staff at the three divisions are involved in the day-to-day running of the savings facilities and their work can include any of the following duties: management, administration, automatic data processing, advertising, planning and policy matters, finance, and communication with the public and with Post Office and bank staff.

The Civil Service

The Department for National Savings is part of the Home Civil Service: that is to say the posts are graded and staff paid according to Civil Service categories and pay scales, and applicants must meet the Civil Service nationality and/or residence requirements. They must be:

(a) British citizens; *or*

(b) Commonwealth citizens (other than British citizens), or British protected persons, or citizens of the Republic of Ireland, in which case they must satisfy one of the following conditions:

  (i) at least one of their parents must be, or have been at death, a Commonwealth citizen, a British protected person, or a citizen of the Republic of Ireland; *or*
  (ii) they must have resided in a country or territory within the Commonwealth, or in the Republic of Ireland, or have been employed elsewhere in the service of the Crown, or partly have so resided and partly been so employed, for at least five years out of the last eight years before the date of appointment; *or*
  (iii) if not qualified under sub-paragraphs (b)(i) or (b)(ii) of this Regulation, they must satisfy the Civil Service Commissioners that they are so closely connected with a country or territory within the Commonwealth either by ancestry, upbringing or residence, or by reason of national service, that an exception may properly be made; *or*.

(c) an EC national.

(Details of additional nationality requirements can be obtained from Recruitment and Assessment Services, Alencon Link, Basingstoke, Hampshire RG21 1JB.)

Recruitment

Jobs are advertised in Jobcentres and in local newspapers; specialist jobs (eg Research Officers) are advertised in the national press and specialist journals. Recruitment is generally at Administrative Assistant level and the following entry requirements may be necessary: two GCSEs (or equivalent) including English language; Administrative Officers require five GCSEs (or equivalent) including English language. National Savings also recruits typists, support staff, information officers, statisticians and graphics officers. There is open competition (ie an entry examination) at Executive Officer level consisting of a written test and panel interview. There is a one-year probationary period during which reports are made on progress after three, five, seven and nine months; thereafter performance is assessed annually.

National Savings is an Equal Opportunity Employer; it also provides part-time and job-sharing work and reinstatement, and employs disabled officers.

Training

There is an on-site induction course for Administrative Assistants which provides an introduction to National Savings conditions of service, union membership and welfare services. Trainees learn about the structure and functions of National Savings and are instructed in the use of the telephone, letter writing and dealing with members of the public. Training is given on the job and is completed in the probationary year. There is an ongoing programme of training courses thereafter.

Promotion

Promotion, which depends on the availability of vacancies, is on merit. In theory it is possible for all civil servants, regardless of their level of entry, to reach the highest grades. National Savings recognises professional qualifications and encourages staff to undertake training to gain qualifications. It is advantageous for those in specialist posts to acquire such professional qualifications as accountancy awards.

Starting Salaries (1994)

	Age 16	*Age 19 (or over)*
Administrative Assistant	£4,995	£6,548
	Age 16	*Age 20 (or over)*
Administrative Officer	£5,529	£8,297
	Age 18	*Age 20 (or over)*
Executive Officer	£8,602	£9,332

Chapter 9

Building Societies

Introduction

The building societies movement is more than 200 years old. For most of that time the societies offered two very basic products: a safe home for savings, and a source of mortgage finance to help people buy their own homes. Most families in the UK have used one or both of these services. Since the Building Societies Act was passed in 1986, the range and variety of services provided by the societies has grown rapidly. The larger societies now compete on equal terms with other players in the financial services league. They provide not only a range of savings accounts, but cheque book facilities, investment advice, life assurance and pensions; some have branched into property services, running their own chain of estate agents as a separate trading operation. Formerly one of the largest societies, Abbey National has become a quoted company, and is legally constituted as a bank. Two other societies, Halifax (the country's largest) and Leeds Permanent, announced at the end of 1994 that, subject to the approval of their members, they are to merge, and will also cease to be mutual societies 'owned' by their depositors and borrowers, but will become instead an independent public company with shares owned by many thousands of investing members of the public, and by institutions such as insurance companies and pension funds. This new bank will be among the largest in Britain, ranking alongside Barclays and NatWest.

The largest societies now have staff experienced in a wide range of services; some were recruited from outside the movement to bring expertise to a rapidly changing movement, but more recently those societies have trained up their traditional staff from within. Now every branch boasts specialists for, say, pensions and credit cards, or unsecured loans, alongside the old skills of granting mortgages, and gathering funds into savings accounts. National and many regional societies offer a cheque book service for personal accounts and a few are starting to compete with the high street banks for small business customers. Some of the smaller societies do not attempt to offer such a comprehensive range of services, and still concentrate on those traditional skills for which the societies are best known.

There are about 80 societies in the UK at present; the number is reducing each year as fresh mergers take place. Each society is an autonomous organisation with its own recruiting policy, training schemes, pay scales and conditions of service; it is worth writing for information to several societies. They vary considerably in size, and obviously the big national societies offer the greatest choice of career opportunities in the long run, but not necessarily the most varied work. Jobs in large societies can be very specialised; in a small society you could find yourself with a greater variety of work. There is some movement of staff, particularly between the smaller societies.

The rapid expansion which followed the freedom to compete granted by the 1986 Act is now behind them; societies have been consolidating, rather than expanding, and mergers and restructuring resulted in some redundancies. However, there is recruitment once again, creating movement within the societies.

Unlike the high street banks, few of the building societies have London head offices; indeed they are based predominantly in the Midlands and the North - Yorkshire is a favoured location. The largest national societies, those with say 300 or more branches, have a structure of head office and regional offices. At the other end of the scale are about 30 societies with fewer than six branches (nine have just a single office). In between are regional societies, represented in a cluster of towns, or in a corner of the country. Some of the smaller societies compete by offering keen interest rates through a specialised postal service and without the cost of running a full national branch network.

For several years the societies have been relying on promotion of existing branch staff to fill management roles, but there is a resumption of highly selective recruitment into management training programmes in some societies. The calibre required is of a good graduate entrant, although suitable experience and maturity gained in other backgrounds may be equally relevant.

Structure

Building societies employ approximately 85,000 people; about

60,000 of them work in branches, the remainder in regional or head offices. Like the high street banks, administration and processing work is often carried out at a centralised location, or a regional service centre.

Most building society branch offices will be staffed by a branch manager, an office manager, one or more trainee managers, interviewers and financial consultants who may be specialists in insurance or investment products, and customer service assistants (cashiers and enquiries staff).

At head office there is a chief executive and a team of senior management. In the larger societies there are specialists in accountancy and finance, insurance, investment management, and personnel and training. Here too will be the centre of computing activities, of mortgage administration, and the legal department. With the expansion of products, marketing support has grown, guiding the societies in promoting new services. The larger societies provide these skills in-house and, like the banks, will operate an advertising department.

The Work

A *branch manager* is responsible for the business handled by the branch and is accountable to regional or head office for the branch's performance. In addition to being responsible for the security of the office and for training and development of the branch staff, it is the manager's role to lead the team in attracting new business. This can include new savings balances and attracting applications for mortgages, as well as the sale of other financial services such as insurance. The manager will become known in the local community, keeping in touch with schools, housing associations and advice centres. For the manager and deputy there can be quite extensive visits outside the office to meet present and potential customers.

The manager sees some of the clients who are applying for mortgages, and will liaise with surveyors, estate agents, solicitors and others involved in the sale and purchase of property. He or she will monitor the preparation of regular statistical returns and information for regional or head office.

Case Study

Bob is the chief executive in a local building society.

I didn't go straight into a building society from school, I spent 12 years in a high street bank. But then two things happened within a few days of each other to make me change course. I read the annual report and accounts of my bank, which ended with the sentence, 'We'd like to thank our 150,000 staff worldwide for all their efforts' and I pictured myself among those 150,000 people and thought, 'Where do I fit into this organisation?' A few days later I saw that a regional building society in the town where I was living was advertising for trainee managers. I went along and met the general manager, who was about 35 years old - I'd been used to dealing with geriatric senior banking types - and he talked me out of a 12-year banking career in about 30 minutes. It was a leap in the dark.

My management career, in fact, goes back to my time with the bank. I left school with five O levels and joined the bank at 16. It was explained to me on day one - the banks are very good at this - that if you want to go places in banking you've got to become an Associate of the Institute of Bankers. It came as quite a shock to me that study did not end when you left school, but having understood that I got down to it and qualified fairly quickly. I was in my late twenties, it was a time when building societies were expanding very rapidly, they were looking for qualified people from outside because they did not have enough trained people to cope with the very rapid growth that was taking place and I was just the sort of person the building societies were looking for. I made a positive decision when I left banking that I was not going to rely on my banking qualifications, so I got down to work very quickly and passed The Chartered Building Societies Institute exams and I think that stood me in good stead.[1]

I spent about three years with the first society and gained a lot of experience in a short time and then I found myself involved with computers. The society, at that time, was the largest non-computerised building society in the country and I joined the team responsible for computerising the society. It was very interesting, but when we'd done it, I wondered if this was really what I wanted to do forever. I'd joined a building society because I wanted to work with people and there I was a member of a small specialist team.

At that point I joined a very small building society, which has now been taken over. It was a tiny organisation, there was a staff of eight and I was the number two. I gained a lot of experience; in about five years I'd seen everything I could possibly see. It was then that I moved to my present society as what in those days was called assistant secretary, the number two. I've been here for nine years now during which time the secretary, who became the general manager, retired and I took over.

I don't see myself moving from here. I've moved around a fair bit,

[1] The Chartered Building Societies Institute merged with the Chartered Institute of Bankers in 1993, and the combined examination syllabus now reflects that change.

moved house a number of times, but the moves took place at a time in my life when they were not disruptive. For the last nine years I've lived in the same house, my children are 10 and 13 and I'm unlikely to have to move in the next five years. If I decide to further my career, I would choose where and when I went. Had I joined one of the national building societies I would have had to go where they sent me. There will certainly be enough challenge because the building society movement is changing so dramatically as a result of the recent Act. It will not be a matter of thinking, 'I've made it to the top, now I can sit back'; there's a lot going on. Building societies are no longer the cosy little organisations they used to be. When I went into the profession we used to change the mortgage rate about once every three years and we knew precisely where we fitted into the market. Suddenly the world has been turned upside down, there are mergers, new powers, new organisations are entering the mortgage market, the competition is very fierce. There's no danger of my stagnating.

We have a management team whose members are responsible for the different sides of the society's work. There's a marketing manager, an administration manager, a financial manager and an internal auditor. Every week I spend a certain amount of time with each of them individually and we have weekly meetings when the whole management team is present. There is a fortnightly board meeting which has to be prepared. We have a personnel officer, but I have overall responsibility for personnel matters and I like to see staff fairly regularly. I spend about one day a month going round the branches or conducting formal staff interviews. We've got a staff of 80, we're like a large family here, and that makes life very interesting. Being in charge of a small society means that I'm very much involved with what's happening in the various departments. I get consulted on everything. Obviously I delegate a lot, but I still know what's going on.

I travel quite a bit. I have to keep up with what's going on in the building society world - and there's a lot going on at the moment - which means attending seminars, usually in London. I represent the society in its regional association and that takes me to London about once a month. I'm very much involved in the professional life of the town, with solicitors, bankers, accountants, surveyors and so on. A lot of co-operation goes on here and I'm very happy with the relationship the society has with its professional contacts. What I like about building society work is that we're in the 'people' business.

Cashiers/customer service assistants undertake a variety of work. It is important that you enjoy meeting people. The duties may include handling investment enquiries, processing new accounts into a computer, checking transactions carried out by standing orders and, for cashiers, balancing the till at the end of the working day.

In some branches there are secretarial staff; in others customer service officers handle their own correspondence. The role of *clerk/typist* in the smaller branch may suit applicants with some audio-typing skills but who seek more varied duties than just secretarial work.

Case Study

Joanne is a customer services officer in a local building society.

> When I was at school I was interested in banks and building societies. I liked the idea of the work, and I wrote round for information. This is my first job and I've been here nearly two years. I came into the society as a junior trainee and did a year's training course going round the various departments. I was trained on the job by people who were doing the work. I went into mortgage administration, investments, data processing and last May I became a cashier. Most of my time now is spent assisting the public, answering queries, plus doing the cashiering side of things. I do some back office work with the ATM, the cash-card machine, ordering cash-cards and balancing the machine every day. I like meeting customers, I like that side of the job. Of course, we do get the occasional irate customer who can be very rude, but you just hold your tongue and put up with it. Most people are very nice. On the whole I enjoy the work very much, just sometimes it's a bit boring when things get very quiet.
>
> I've passed the Certificate, the first exam, and I'm enrolled to take the Associateship. I've got all my study books and I'm hoping to take the first two exams in November. I may do all my studying at home but for the Certificate I attended evening classes. But, yes, you do need to be motivated. I want a career, I want to get as far as I can – to supervisory level or management, or I may move to a larger society. I worked for my A levels and I want to do something with my professional qualifications.

Entry and Training

Most people join a building society at the age of 18. Entry requirements vary from society to society and, although some do not stipulate any minimum academic qualifications, in these competitive times it is a good idea to offer a number of well-balanced GCSEs (or equivalent) including mathematics and English. All societies attach great importance to personal qualities: numeracy, integrity and good communication skills are high on their list of priorities. A-level entrants can rise to managerial posts and graduates are being recruited in increasing numbers to train for head office and managerial posts.

Building societies have a good record for staff training and a tradition of promoting from within the organisation. On-the-job training is designed to give experience of all aspects of branch work and employees can make up their minds which aspects of the work attract them most. Many become assistant managers in their early twenties and managers of large branches by their mid-thirties. Societies run courses at in-house training centres, use computer-based and video training packages and send employees on courses. The big societies, obviously, have more extensive programmes than the smaller ones.

Annual Starting Salaries

There is no standard scale, but a national society quoted starting salaries as:

Customer service advisers: £6,500 to £7,000, or more for relevant experience
Graduates can expect £12,500 to £13,000.

For those working in central London, a London weighting allowance of £3,000 is representative, and there may be smaller allowances for certain large towns.

The Building Societies Association's members are the societies. It acts on their behalf, representing them to Government, Parliament, and the media. Also the Association will provide schools and colleges, and potential employees, with information about the industry in general (addresses on pp. 106–10).

Since 1993 the Chartered Institute of Bankers has been the professional body for both bank and building society staff. It is the certificating body for professional examinations. For details see Chapter 11.

Chapter 10

Getting a Job

Introduction

Whether you are a graduate, school- or college-leaver or job changer, you are likely to face competition when you apply for almost any job; for some posts the competition is very stiff. Most bankers start their career in branch banking, but do not forget the other opportunities that exist for entrants of all levels. This chapter deals with how to present yourself on paper and in person.

How and When to Apply

Do not wait for the results of your examinations. If you are applying for a clerical post write as soon as you know which GCSE (or equivalent) or A-level (or equivalent) subjects you will be taking.

You may be thinking of going on to further education before applying for a job; if so, talk over with your careers teacher the pros and cons of starting work immediately or of trying to improve your qualifications. If you are applying to one of the high street banks, find out whether you should write to the central personnel office, to the nearest area office, or to one of its specialist divisions. If you are applying to a building society, write to the personnel officer at the society's head office (see pp. 106–10).

Those studying for a degree should apply early in their final year. Your university careers office will have details of careers and recruitment literature. It will also tell you if and when recruiting visits (the 'Milk Round') will be made. Those who graduated some time ago should apply direct to the bank(s) of their choice.

The employers described in this book sometimes use the local press to advertise specific posts. Reply to such advertisements in the way they specify (ie make a telephone call, send a CV, write for application form etc).

Letters of Application

It is important to write a good letter of application because your letter will be one of the things which determines whether or not an employer will interview you.

- ☐ Don't write the story of your life - put brief details of exams, certificates, achievements etc, on a CV.
- ☐ Keep your letter short and to the point.
- ☐ Say why you want the job.
- ☐ Make a rough copy and show it to your careers teacher or your parents.
- ☐ Make sure there are no spelling mistakes or grammatical errors in your letter. If you are in doubt ask someone who is good at English to look it over for you.
- ☐ Write clearly and neatly on plain white paper.

Curriculum Vitae (CV)

If you are applying for a job you should draw up a CV. It would be money well spent to have this typed professionally. Keep the master copy clean and make photocopies to send off with your application. A specimen CV is shown opposite.

- ☐ Do not exaggerate or make false claims on your CV (or on an application form); these will probably be discovered at an interview.
- ☐ Leave out any heading under which you have nothing to list (eg previous employment).
- ☐ Your referees should be people in authority or in a responsible position (eg a head teacher, youth leader, GP) who know you reasonably well but are not related to you.

Make a note of all your applications; it is useful to keep a progress chart of the stage each has reached, recording date of application, date and nature of reply, interview arrangements etc. You should also have a file for each of your applications containing correspondence, company literature, notes you make about the company and your reasons for applying and any other relevant information. It is particularly important to keep this sort of filing system; it will help you to perform well at interviews and make a generally good impression.

JOHN NEIL SMITH
11 BOLTON STREET, BRISTOL BS3 4AL
Tel: BRISTOL 59178

DATE OF BIRTH . . . . AGE NOW: . . . .

EDUCATION: (From) –
(Names of schools/colleges and towns) (To)

(List schools, colleges, university, including institutions where you have studied part-time)

QUALIFICATIONS:
(Number and names of exams) (Subjects)

(Group school exams together, eg four GCSE passes – English, biology, maths, geography – with grades. List any subsequent examinations separately)

PREVIOUS EMPLOYMENT (include Saturday and holiday jobs): (Position) (From) –
(Name of company/employer and town) (To)

OTHER ACTIVITIES:
(It is best to list only specific positions or achievements or one or two sports or club memberships which are important to you or relevant. But it is useful to list anything that indicates qualities such as leadership or responsibility, eg youth leader)

REFERENCES: (Name) (Occupation)
(1)
(2)
(3)

Sample layout for a curriculum vitae

Filling in an Application Form

No matter how detailed your CV, you will probably be asked to fill in an application form.

- ☐ Write clearly and neatly in ink.
- ☐ Follow the instructions carefully.
- ☐ Answer the questions exactly; if you don't understand a question, ask your parents or a teacher.
- ☐ Read the advertisement and any company literature you can find to get a picture of what the employer is looking for.

- ☐ Put dashes where questions do not apply to you, to show that you have not ignored or missed them.
- ☐ Make a draft of answers to such questions as: 'What factors have influenced your choice of employment?' or 'How do you think this post will satisfy your ambitions?' or 'What do you see yourself doing in five years from now?'
- ☐ Make a photocopy of the completed form so that before an interview you can remind yourself what information you have supplied.

Note: You will probably find a question about your racial origins on a bank's application form. The Commission for Racial Equality has drawn up the following categories:

Black - Afro-Caribbean, African, Asian, other
White - UK/Eire, other European, other

and you could be asked to 'put a tick in the appropriate box'. The banks are equal opportunity employers, that is to say they seek to provide equal opportunities for all staff regardless of race, sex, religion or marital status, and claim that, though answers to this question play no part in the selection process, they need the information in order to monitor the effectiveness of their policy as recommended by the Commission's Code of Practice for the Elimination of Racial Discrimination and Promotion of Equal Opportunity in Employment, which came into force on 1 April 1984.

The Interview

Interviews may make you nervous, but remember most people feel nervous no matter how many interviews they have been through. Try not to show your nerves. Don't always answer with a simple 'yes' or 'no'; enlarge on what you said on the application form. You will probably be asked such questions as 'Why do you want this job?', 'Why have you chosen banking (or building society work)?', 'Do you enjoy working with figures, using words, operating machines?', 'What are your ambitions?' so think out how you might answer them. And remember to:

- ☐ Arrive on time. Set out early for your bus or train and allow plenty of time for finding the place where the interview is to be held.
- ☐ Look clean and neat - bankers and building society

employees dress in a rather conservative manner; some even wear a uniform.

- ☐ Sound as if you want the job.
- ☐ Shake hands firmly and look the interviewer(s) in the eye.

Finally, remember that an interview is not just a matter of *answering* questions. You will probably be invited to *ask* questions and if you have none it could indicate a lack of interest. A prospective employee wants to know about such things as: salary, training, recreational facilities, promotion prospects.

Training for Work

Training for Work is just one of the schemes offered through the Department of Employment. Anyone aged from 18 to 59 who has been unemployed for six months or more is eligible to enter this programme. Priority is given to those who have been out of work for 12 months, and have been through a Jobplan Workshop, or for those who are unemployed and disabled.

The scheme is designed to help unemployed adults to train or gain useful work experience which is directly related to the job they wish to do. After an initial assessment they are given guidance to make sure that the programme is tailored to their individual needs. It may take the form of job-specific training, work towards a National Vocational Qualification (NVQ), work preparation, temporary work to keep skills up-to-date, or a mixture of these schemes. Participants will continue to receive their usual benefit, plus a small supplement, and possibly help with travelling and other out-of-pocket expenses.

Other schemes available include Learning for Work, Open Learning, and training for young people (16 and 17 year olds) through the Youth Training scheme. For details contact your local Jobcentre.

Part 2

Chapter 11

The Chartered Institute of Bankers

Introduction

The Institute was founded in 1879 and now has a membership of around 90,000. It produces a monthly journal, runs 97 local centres, holds seminars and courses on a wide range of banking and financial services topics, and publishes books and guides of interest to the practitioner. It is the certificating body for professional examinations in banking and building society work, having merged with the Chartered Building Societies Institute in 1993.

Fellows (FCIB) are elected by the Council from Associates of managerial status. Associates (ACIB) are Members who have passed the Associateship examinations and who have been employed in banking or related work and have been Members of the Institute for not less than three years. Ordinary Membership is open to all.

At whatever level you enter banking you may be encouraged to become a Member of the Institute and, after completing a probationary period, to sit its examinations. If you want a career post it is helpful to acquire a professional qualification.

The Certificate in Financial Services Practice

This is a first-level course (no entry qualifications) for customer contact staff. Originally designed for those in building societies, it is being relaunched in January 1995 and will include banking modules for the first time. To qualify for the certificate, candidates are required to build up eight credits from the range available which must include the double module, The Financial Services Industry and its Environment. Each module has its own study manual produced by the CIB.

The Banking Certificate

This is a three-year course which has a strong work-related element. Year one (Preliminary section) is open to all, whatever their qualifications, and includes the study of business calculations, business communications and the business of banking. It leads to the Final section which covers the subjects: economics and the banks' role in the economy; introduction to accounting; banking - the legal environment; supervisory skills; bank operations - UK lending and international business; and customer services - marketing and the competitive environment. If you have one or more A levels and a GCSE (or equivalent) pass in English or five years' relevant work experience, you may enter the Final Section directly.

Pre-Associateship Route

Students who obtain three merit passes in the Preliminary section at one sitting or who hold an A level and GCSE in English can choose to take the Pre-Associateship Route instead of entering the Final section. This is not a qualification in its own right but enables you to sit the Associateship examinations.

Associateship Examinations

If you wish to go into management you are advised to continue your studies and gain the Associateship of the Chartered Institute of Bankers. This usually takes about three years' part-time study and covers four core areas: law relating to banking services; the monetary and financial system; accountancy; and management. There are also four optional subjects chosen from a list of 17 which reflect likely career paths and, following the merger with the CBSI, now include building society options.

Routes into the Associateship examinations, apart from the Banking Certificate or successful completion of the Pre-Associateship Route, are the BTEC National Diploma in Business and Finance, a recognised degree or a professional qualification.

Post-Associateship

The Lombard Scheme is a new programme leading to the award of a Master's Degree in Business Administration (MBA). It is designed for those seeking to reach senior management and involves considerable commitment.

The CIB has recently launched the *Degree Partnership Pro-*

gramme, which allows Associates to 'top up' their professional qualification to honours degree status at selected universities.

Methods of Study

Tuition is available at approximately 100 colleges of further and higher education in England and Wales, and many banks and building societies grant employees study leave and assist with study costs. If there are no college courses available in your area you can study by correspondence course.

There are also flexible learning schemes, Computer-assisted Learning (CAL) and the Chartered Institute of Bankers' Local Centre Revision Courses.

For further information about membership of the Institute, qualifications, regulations and syllabuses, and colleges offering approved courses, write to The Membership Services Unit, The Chartered Institute of Bankers, Emmanuel House, 4–9 Burgate Lane, Canterbury CT1 2XJ.

Chapter 12

The Chartered Institute of Bankers in Scotland

Introduction

The Chartered Institute of Bankers in Scotland is a professional body for employees in the financial services sector in Scotland. It was founded in 1875 and has a membership of 13,000. It publishes a quarterly journal *The Scottish Banker*, runs 12 District Centres, holds seminars and courses on a wide range of banking topics and publishes books and guides of interest to the practising banker and others employed in the financial services section. It is the certificating body for the Scottish professional examinations in banking and financial services. Employees of all levels are encouraged to work for the Institute's awards which are available on a distance learning block-release basis.

Fellows (FCIBS) are elected by Council in recognition of a significant contribution made to banking or the Institute.

Courses and Qualifications

Stage 1: Certificate in Financial Services

This is a new stand-alone qualification which is offered on a distance learning basis. It has been designed to assist in meeting the basic practical job needs of large numbers of staff in the financial services sector. There are 11 subject units of which students have to complete six to gain the award of the Certificate. These units are: Introduction to Financial Services, Basic Accounting and Tax, Economic Environment, Legal Environment, Banking Operations, Introduction to Investment, Mortgage Lending, Sales and Service, Team Participation and Development, Information Technology and Introduction to Insurance. Students are assessed on a continuous basis and by a final examination. Students wishing to progress to the Associateship course must take the first four units from the above list.

Stage 2: The Associateship Course

Associateship Course (ACIBS) usually lasts for three years and tuition is provided by means of a combined home-study distance-learning course and block-release tuition at one of a number of financial studies learning centres located throughout Scotland. The four main Scottish banks have made arrangements to reimburse staff in respect of fees and distance-learning materials. The Associateship qualification is awarded to those who have passed examinations in: Practical Banking 1 and 2; Law of Banking; Monetary Economics; Business Accounting; Marketing; Investment; Management; Foreign Business; and Taxation. The Associateship may only be taken by those holding a higher preliminary qualification, ie a UK degree or a Higher National Certificate/Diploma or the Certificate in Financial Services.

Stage 3: The Members Course

The Members Course was introduced in September 1992 and tuition is by means of block-release study at further/higher education institutions. To qualify for the award of MCIBS students must pass four of the following subjects including the two core subjects:

Core subjects
Strategic management and marketing
Financial management

Elective subjects
Management and business
Corporate finance
International banking and finance
European Union and international business.

College Courses

Tuition for the Chartered Institute of Bankers in Scotland courses is available at universities and further education colleges throughout Scotland.

Further details are available from the Chartered Institute of Bankers in Scotland (address on p. 99).

Distance Learning Courses

All distance learning courses are administered and run by the Chartered Institute of Bankers in Scotland.

Chapter 13

The Finance & Leasing Association

Introduction

The Finance & Leasing Association (FLA) was formed in January 1992 by the merger of the Equipment Leasing Association and the Finance Houses Association. It represents the interests of companies offering business finance and leasing, consumer credit and motor finance. The FLA works to promote high standards of lending and leasing, to safeguard the interests of its members and to ensure their views are heard.

The Examinations

The FLA Examination Council is responsible for the administration of the Diploma Examinations and for maintaining the academic standards of the Diploma and Higher Diploma Examinations undertaken by personnel operating in the finance and leasing industry. The Diploma with merit is the equivalent of a second year Bachelor of Commerce (Hons) degree.

The Diploma

The Finance & Leasing Association Diploma Examination is in two parts and is open to all, whether from a member or non-member company. Part One comprises: elements of financial appraisal; general principles of law; and elements of finance and leasing. Part Two covers the law and practice of credit and leasing. Candidates are required to pass one of the three options, which cater for staff operating in traditional consumer credit business, corporate lending and leasing, or credit cards. Part Two comprises two three-hour papers from: consumer credit; business finance and leasing; credit cards; and business credit financial appraisal. The two papers to be taken will depend on which option is selected by the candidate.

The Higher Diploma is available for Diploma holders who wish to widen their technical knowledge by studying the two subjects not taken in obtaining the Diploma. It also provides a useful course of study for those engaged in other forms of banking and finance. Tuition is by correspondence course provided by The Rapid Results College, Tuition House, 27–37 St George's Road, London SW19 4DS, and the Association runs residential revision courses (not a substitute for the correspondence course) approximately six weeks before the examination.

Training Courses

The FLA runs a number of residential training courses at Basic Leasing, Intermediate Leasing, and Senior Leasing levels, as well as courses on Consumer Credit. These are open to members and non-members alike, and are based on practical work, with syndicate exercises forming an important part of the courses.

Further information on the examinations and training courses can be obtained from the Finance & Leasing Association (address on p. 101).

Chapter 14

Awards from Institutions of Higher Education

Universities offering Bachelors' Degrees in Banking and Finance or Financial Services

Birmingham University	BSocSci Money, Banking & Finance
Bournemouth University	BA Financial Services
University of Central England, Birmingham	BA Financial Services
City University	BSc Banking and International Finance
University of Central Lancashire	BA Financial Services
Loughborough University	BSc Banking & Finance
Sheffield Hallam University	BA Hons Financial Services
Portsmouth University	BA Hons Financial Services
Ulster University	BA Banking & Finance
University of Wales, Bangor	BA Banking Insurance and Finance
University of Wales, Cardiff	BSc Banking & Finance
University of the West of England	BA Hons Financial Services

There are also a number of universities offering degrees in accounting and finance.

Chapter 15

Addresses and Sources of Useful Information

General

Banking Information Service, 10 Lombard Street, London EC3V 9AT

Chartered Institute of Bankers, 90 Bishopsgate, London EC2N 4AS (For information about membership, qualifications, regulations and syllabuses, colleges offering approved courses, write to The Registrar, Chartered Institute of Bankers, Emmanuel House, 4-9 Burgate Lane, Canterbury CT1 2XJ.)

The Chartered Institute of Bankers in Scotland, 19 Rutland Square, Edinburgh EH1 2DE

The Institute of Bankers in Ireland, Nassau House, Nassau Street, Dublin 2

The Bank of England

The Bank of England, Personnel Division (BB-1), 1-2 Bank Buildings, Princes Street, London EC2R 8EU. Write to the Manager (Recruiting).

The High Street Banks

Abbey National, Abbey House, 201 Grafton Gate East, Central Milton Keynes MK9 1AN. Write to the Personnel Manager or Graduate Recruitment Manager.

Bank of Scotland, Personnel Division, Teviot House, PO Box 475, 41 South Gyle Crescent, Edinburgh EH12 9DR. Write to Personnel Division. IT enquiries also to this address; graduates should write to the bank's Training and Management Development Department, 58-62 St Alban's Road, Edinburgh EH9 2LS.

Barclays Bank, Barclays House, 1 Wimborne Road, Poole, Dorset BH15 2BB. Write to The Resourcing & Selection Manager. Graduates should write to PO Box 256, Fleetway House, 25 Farringdon Street, London EC4A 4LP. Enquiries about computer work in centres in London,

Gloucester and South Manchester should be addressed to The Head of Personnel, Barclays Bank, Radbroke Hall, Knutsford, Cheshire WA16 9EU.

Clydesdale Bank, 150 Buchanan Street, Glasgow G1 2HL. Write to the Personnel Manager. Computer enquiries to Human Resources Manager, National Australia Group, 3rd Floor, Guildhall, 57 Queen Street, Glasgow G1 1TB.

The Co-operative Bank, 1 Balloon Street, Manchester M60 4EP. Write to the Human Resources Manager. Enquiries about computer work, and by graduates, should be sent to the above address.

Coutts & Co, 190 Fleet Street, London EC4A 2HT. Write to The Personnel Manager for general, graduate, or IT information.

Lloyds Bank, Recruitment Administration Unit, 8–10 Waterloo Place, London SW1Y 4BH. Write to the Recruitment Manager. Graduate enquiries should be sent to 46–48 Park Street, London SE1 9EQ; IT applicants should write to Systems & Support, also at Park Street.

Midland Bank (Recruitment Manager), Griffin House, Silver Street Head, Sheffield S1 3GG. Alternatively ask your local branch to put you in touch with the area office. Graduate and IT enquiries should be made to the Sheffield address.

National Westminster Bank, 5th Floor, Cavell House, 2a Charing Cross Road, London WC2H 0NN. Write to the Recruitment Manager or Graduate Recruitment Manager. IT applications should be made to PO Box 114, Goodmans Fields, 71 Alie Street, London E1 8HI.

The Royal Bank of Scotland, Regent's House, 42 Islington High Street, London N1 8XL. Write to the Personnel Manager or ask the local branch to put you in touch with the area office. The computer centres are in London and Edinburgh; enquiries about computer work and applications by graduates should be sent to the above address.

TSB Bank, Victoria House, Victoria Square, Birmingham B1 1BZ. Write to the Manager Recruitment & Selection, or to Management & Graduate Recruitment, as appropriate. For IT centres in Manchester and Milton Keynes, contact Personnel Technology at Southgate Centre 1, 319 Wilmslow Road, Heald Green, Cheadle, Cheshire SK8 3NW.

Yorkshire Bank, 20 Merrion Way, Leeds LS2 8NZ. All applicants should write to Recruitment & Selection, including those for IT vacancies in Leeds.

In all cases, enquiries about local vacancies should be made to a bank's regional office; you can find out the name and address of the person to write to at any local branch.

Girobank

Girobank plc, Bootle, Merseyside GIR 0AA. For details about the Management Trainee Programme write to The Personnel Department.

Credit Card Processing Companies

Barclaycard, Northampton NN1 1SG

First Data Resources, FDR House, Christopher Martin Road, Basildon SS14 9AA

Merchant Banks

London Investment Banking Association, 6 Frederick's Place, London EC2R 8BT. The Association will supply a list of its members. Write to The Secretary.

Finance Houses and Leasing Companies

Finance & Leasing Association, 18 Upper Grosvenor Street, London W1X 9PB. Tel: 0171 491 2783. Fax: 0171 629 0396. The Association will supply a list of its members.

International Banks

The Clearing Banks

Write for information to the general or graduate recruitment departments listed on pages 99 and 100, except for:

Midland Bank, write to parent company, Hongkong and Shanghai Banking Corporation group (see below).

TSB Bank, International Division, Henry Duncan House, 120 George Street, Edinburgh EH2 4TS

Other International Banks

Standard Chartered Bank, 1 Aldermanbury Square, London EC2V 7SB

The Hongkong and Shanghai Banking Corporation. Write to HSBC Holdings, 10 Lower Thames Street, London EC3R 6AE.

Foreign Banks

There are over 400 foreign banks in London, many of them with very few staff. Those listed below employ 100 or more people, but there are a number of banks with staff numbers just below that level. You should research thoroughly if you are interested in a particular country or geographical area. *The Banker* magazine (Greystoke Place, Fetter Lane, London EC4A 1ND) publishes a comprehensive list annually, normally in November. I am grateful to the publishers for permission to quote from their survey.

Australia

ANZ Banking Group, Minerva House, PO Box 7, Montague Close, London SE1 9DA

Commonwealth Bank of Australia, Senator House, 85 Queen Victoria Street, London EC4V 4HA

National Australia Bank, 6–8 Tokenhouse Yard, London EC2R 7AJ

Westpac Banking Corporation, 75 King William Street, London EC4N 7HA

Austria

Creditanstalt-Bankverein, 125 London Wall, London EC2Y 5DD

Bahrain

ABC International Bank, 1–5 Moorgate, London EC2R 6AB

Canada

Bank of Montreal, 11 Walbrook, London EC4N 8ED

Bank of Nova Scotia, 33 Finsbury Square, London EC2A 1BB

Canadian Imperial Bank of Commerce, Cottons Centre, Cottons Lane, London SE1 2QL

Royal Bank of Canada, 71 Queen Victoria Street, London EC4V 4DE

China

Bank of China, 90 Cannon Street, London EC4N 6HA

Cyprus

Bank of Cyprus (London), 27–31 Charlotte Street, London W1P 2HJ

Cyprus Popular Bank, 19 Fitzroy Street, London W1P 6BQ

Denmark

Den Danske Bank, 75 King William Street, London EC4N 7DT

Finland

Merita Bank, 19 Thomas More Street, London EC4N 6JJ

France
Banque Indosuez, 122 Leadenhall Street, London EC3V 4QH

Banque Nationale de Paris, 8-13 King William Street, London EC4P 4HS

Crédit Lyonnais, 84-94 Queen Victoria Street, London EC4P 4LX

Paribas, 33 Wigmore Street, London W1H 0BN

Société Générale, Exchange House, Primrose Street, Broadgate, London EC2A 2DD

Germany
Commerzbank, 23 Austin Friars, London EC2P 2JD

Deutsche Bank AG, 6 Bishopsgate, London EC2P 2AT

Deutsche Morgan Grenfell, 23 Great Winchester Street, London EC2P 2AX

Dresdner Bank, 125 Wood Street, London EC2V 7AQ

Westdeutsche Landesbank Girozentrale, 51 Moorgate, London EC2R 6AE

Greece
National Bank of Greece, 50 St Mary Axe, London EC3A 8EL

India
Bank of Baroda, 31-32 King Street, London EC2V 8EN

State Bank of India, 1 Milk Street, London EC2P 2JP

Ireland
Allied Irish Bank, Bankcentre Britain, Belmont Road, Uxbridge, Middlesex UB8 1SA

Bank of Ireland, 34 High Street, Slough, Berkshire SL1 1ED

Israel
Bank Leumi (UK), 4-7 Woodstock Street, London W1A 2AF

Italy
Banca Commerciale Italiana, 42 Gresham Street, London EC2V 7LA

Banca di Roma, 81-87 Gresham Street, London EC2V 7NQ

Banca Nazionale del Lavoro, Fitzwilliam House, 10 St Mary Axe, London EC3V 3QD

Credito Italiano, 17 Moorgate, London EC2R 6AR

Istituto Bancario San Paulo di Torino, 15 Carter Lane, London EC4V 5SP

Japan

Bank of Tokyo, 12–15 Finsbury Circus, London EC2M 7BT

Dai-Ichi Kangyo Bank, 24 King William Street, London EC4R 9DB

Daiwa Europe Bank, 14 St Paul's Churchyard, London EC4M 8BD

Fuji Bank, 7–11 Finsbury Circus, London EC2M 7DH

Guinness Mahon & Co, 32 St Mary at Hill, London EC3P 3AJ

Industrial Bank of Japan/IBJ International, 1 Friday Street, London EC4M 9JA

Long Term Credit Bank of Japan, 55 Bishopsgate, London EC2Y 5AH

Mitsubishi Bank, 6 Broadgate, London EC2M 2SX

Nikko Bank (UK) 17 Godliman Street, London EC4V 5BD

Nomura Bank International (UK), 1 St Martins Le Grand, London EC1A 4NP

Sakura Bank, 6 Broadgate, London EC2M 2RQ

Sanwa Bank, 55 Basinghall Street, London EC2V 5DL

Sumitomo Bank, Temple Court, 11 Queen Victoria Street, London EC4N 4TA

Tokai Bank, One Exchange Square, London EC4N 8EL

Tokai Bank Europe, 14 Finsbury Square, London EC2A 1DR

Jordan

Arab Bank, 15 Moorgate, London EC2R 6LP

Kuwait

National Bank of Kuwait International, 13 George Street, London W1H 5PB

United Bank of Kuwait, 7 Baker Street, London W1M 1AB

Netherlands

ABN-AMRO Bank, 101 Moorgate, London EC2M 6SB

ING Bank, 60 London Wall, London EC2M 5TQ

Rabobank Nederland, 108 Cannon Street, London EC4N 6RN

Norway
Den Norske Bank, 20 St Dunstan's Hill, London EC3R 8HY

Pakistan
Habib Bank, 97 Cannon Street, London EC4N 5AD

Russia
Moscow Narodny Bank, 81 King William Street, London EC4P 4JS

Saudi Arabia
Saudi International Bank, One Knightsbridge, London SW1X 7XS

South Africa
Standard Bank London, 25 Dowgate Hill, London EC4R 2SB

Spain
Banco Bilbao Vizcaya, 100 Cannon Street, London EC4N 6EH

Sweden
Skandinaviska Enskilda Banken, 2–6 Cannon Street, London EC4M 6XX

Svenska Handelsbanken, 3–5 Newgate Street, London EC1A 7DA

Switzerland
Credit Suisse, 5 Cabot Square, London EC2N 4BQ

SBC Warburg, 1 Finsbury Avenue, London EC4V 3SB

Union Bank of Switzerland, 100 Liverpool Street, EC2M 2RH

United States of America
American Express Bank, 60 Buckingham Palace Road, London SW1W 0RR

BankAmerica Corporation, 1 Alie Street, London E1 8DE

Bankers Trust Company, 1 Appold Street, Broadgate, London EC2A 2HE

Bank of New York Company, 46 Berkeley Street, London W1X 6AA

Chase Manhattan Bank and Chase Investment Bank, Woolgate House, Coleman Street, London EC2P 2HD

Chemical Bank, 125 London Wall, London EC2Y 5AJ

Citibank, 336 Strand, London WC2R 1HB

First National Bank of Boston, 39 Victoria Street, London SW1H 0ED

First National Bank of Chicago, 90 Long Acre, Covent Garden, London WC2E 9RB

Goldman Sachs, 133 Fleet Street, London EC4A 2BB

Mellon Bank, 1 Suffolk Lane, London EC4R 0AN

Merrill Lynch International Bank, 33 Chester Street, London SW1X 7XD

JP Morgan, 60 Victoria Embankment, London EC4Y 0JP

NationsBank of North Carolina, 35 New Broad Street, London EC2M 1NH

Northern Trust Company, 155 Bishopsgate, London EC2M 3XS

Republic National Bank of New York, 30 Monument Street, London EC3R 8NB

Riggs AP Bank, 21 Great Winchester Street, London EC2N 2HH

State Street Bank & Trust, 1 Royal Exchange Steps, Royal Exchange, London EC3V 3LE

Civil Service

Civil Service Commission, Alencon Link, Basingstoke, Hampshire RG21 1JB

Department for National Savings, Charles House, 375 Kensington High Street, London W14 8SD. Write to The Establishment Officer.

The Building Societies

The Building Societies Association, 3 Savile Row, London W1X 1AF

The Societies[1]

Alliance & Leicester Building Society, 49 Park Lane, London W1Y 4EQ

Barnsley Building Society, Permanent Building, Regent Street, Barnsley, South Yorkshire S70 2EH

Bath Investment and Building Society, 20 Charles Street, Bath BA1 1HY

Beverley Building Society, 57 Market Place, Beverley, Humberside HU17 8AA

Birmingham Midshires Building Society, PO Box 81, Pendleford Business Park, Wobaston Road, Wolverhampton WV1 1EL

[1] These societies are all members of the BSA. The only authorised society not a BSA member is the Century Building Society.

Bradford & Bingley Building Society, PO Box 88, Crossflatts, Bingley, West Yorkshire BD16 2UA

Bristol & West Building Society, Broad Quay, Bristol BS99 7AX

Britannia Building Society, Britannia House, Leek, Staffordshire ST13 5RG

Buckinghamshire Building Society, High Street, Chalfont St Giles, Buckinghamshire HP8 4BQ

Cambridge Building Society, 32 St Andrew's Street, Cambridge CB2 3AR

Catholic Building Society, 7 Strutton Ground, London SW1P 2HY

Chelsea Building Society, Thirlestaine Hall, Thirlestaine Road, Cheltenham, Gloucestershire GL53 7AL

Chesham Building Society, 12 Market Square, Chesham, Buckinghamshire HP5 1ER

Cheshire Building Society, Castle Street, Macclesfield, Cheshire SK11 6AH

Chorley & District Building Society, Key House, Foxhole Road, Chorley, Lancashire PR7 1NZ

City & Metropolitan Building Society, 219 High Street, Bromley, Kent BR1 1PR

Clay Cross Benefit Building Society, Eyre Street, Clay Cross, Chesterfield S45 9NS

Coventry Building Society, Economic House, PO Box 9, High Street, Coventry CV1 5QN

Cumberland Building Society, Cumberland House, Castle Street, Carlisle, Cumbria CA3 8RX

Darlington Building Society, Sentinel House, Lingfield Way, Darlington, Co Durham DL1 4PR

Derbyshire Building Society, PO Box 1, Duffield Hall, Duffield, Derby DE56 1AG

Dudley Building Society, Dudley House, Stone Street, Dudley, West Midlands DY1 1NP

Dunfermline Building Society, Caledonia House, Carnegie Avenue, Dunfermline KY11 5PJ

Earl Shilton Building Society, 22 The Hollow, Earl Shilton, Leicester LE9 7NB

Ecology Building Society, 18 Station Road, Cross Hills, Nr Keighley, West Yorkshire BD20 7EH

Furness Building Society, 51-55 Duke Street, Barrow-in-Furness LA14 1RT

Gainsborough Building Society, Marshall House, 9 Lord Street, Gainsborough, Lincolnshire DN21 2DD

Greenwich Building Society, 279-283 Greenwich High Road, London SE10 8NL

Halifax Building Society, PO Box 60, Trinity Road, Halifax HX1 2RG

Hanley Economic Building Society, Granville House, Festival Park, Hanley, Stoke on Trent ST1 5TB

Harpenden Building Society, 14-16 Station Road, Harpenden, Hertfordshire AL5 4SE

Hinckley and Rugby Building Society, Upper Bond Street, Hinckley, Leicestershire LE10 1DG

Holmesdale Building Society, 43 Church Street, Reigate, Surrey RH2 0AE

Ilkeston Permanent Building Society, 24-26 South Street, Ilkeston, Derbyshire DE7 5HQ

Ipswich Building Society, 44 Upper Brook Street, Ipswich, Suffolk IP4 1DP

Kent Reliance Building Society, Reliance House, Manor Road, Chatham, Kent ME4 6AF

Lambeth Building Society, 118-120 Westminster Bridge Road, London SE1 7XE

Leeds & Holbeck Building Society, 105 Albion Street, Leeds LS1 5AS

Leek United Building Society, 50 St Edward Street, Leek, Staffordshire ST13 5DH

Londonderry Provident Building Society, 31A Carlisle Road, Londonderry BT48 6JJ

Loughborough Building Society, 6 High Street, Loughborough, Leicestershire LE11 2QB

Manchester Building Society, 18-20 Bridge Street, Manchester M3 3BU

Mansfield Building Society, Regent House, Regent Street, Mansfield, Nottinghamshire NG18 1SS

Market Harborough Building Society, Welland House, The Square, Market Harborough, Leicestershire LE16 7PD

Marsden Building Society, 6-20 Russell Street, Nelson, Lancashire BB9 7NJ

Melton Mowbray Building Society, 39 Nottingham Street, Melton Mowbray, Leicestershire LE13 1NR

Mercantile Building Society, Mercantile House, Silverlink, Wallsend, Tyne & Wear NE28 2NY

Monmouthshire Building Society, John Frost Square, Newport, Gwent NP9 1PX

National Counties Building Society, Church Street, Epsom, Surrey KT17 4NL

National & Provincial Building Society, Provincial House, Bradford BD1 1NL

Nationwide Building Society, Nationwide House, Pipers Way, Swindon SN38 1NW

Newbury Building Society, 17–20 Bartholomew Street, Newbury, Berkshire RG14 5LY

Newcastle Building Society, Portland House, New Bridge Street, Newcastle upon Tyne NE1 8AL

Northern Rock Building Society, Northern Rock House, Gosforth, Newcastle upon Tyne NE3 4PL

Norwich & Peterborough Building Society, Peterborough Business Park, Lynch Wood, Peterborough PE2 6WZ

Nottingham Building Society, Nottingham House, 5–13 Upper Parliament Street, Nottingham NG1 2BX

Nottingham Imperial Building Society, Imperial House, 72 Bridgford Road, West Bridgford, Nottingham NG2 6AP

Penrith Building Society, 7 King Street, Penrith, Cumbria CA11 7AR

Portman Building Society, Portman House, Richmond Hill, Bournemouth, Dorset BH2 6EP

Principality Building Society, Principality Buildings, PO Box 89, Queen Street, Cardiff CF1 1UA

Progressive Building Society, 33–37 Wellington Place, Belfast BT1 6HH

Saffron Walden, Herts & Essex Building Society, Saffron House, 1A Market Street, Saffron Walden, Essex CB10 1HX

Scarborough Building Society, Prospect House, PO Box 6, Scarborough, North Yorkshire YO12 6EQ

Scottish Building Society, 23 Manor Place, Edinburgh EH3 7XE

Shepshed Building Society, Bull Ring, Shepshed, Loughborough, Leicestershire LE12 9QD

Skipton Building Society, The Bailey, Skipton, North Yorkshire BD23 1DN

Stafford Railway Building Society, 4 Market Square, Stafford ST16 2JH

Staffordshire Building Society, Jubilee House, PO Box 66, 84 Salop Street, Wolverhampton WV3 0SA

Standard Building Society, 64 Church Way, North Shields, Tyne & Wear NE29 0AF

Stroud & Swindon Building Society, Rowcroft, Stroud, Gloucestershire GL5 3BG

Swansea Building Society, 11 Craddock Street, Swansea SA1 3EW

Teachers' Building Society, Allenview House, Hanham Road, Wimborne, Dorset BH21 1AG

Tipton & Coseley Building Society, 70 Owen Street, Tipton, West Midlands DY4 8HG

Universal Building Society, Universal House, Kings Manor, Newcastle upon Tyne NE1 6PA

Vernon Building Society, 19 St Petersgate, Stockport, Cheshire SK1 1HF

West Bromwich Building Society, 374 High Street, West Bromwich, West Midlands B70 8LR

West Cumbria Building Society, Cumbria House, Murray Road, Workington CA14 2AD

Woolwich Building Society, Corporate Headquarters, Watling Street, Bexleyheath, Kent DA6 7RR

Yorkshire Building Society, Yorkshire House, Yorkshire Drive, Bradford BD5 8LJ

Chapter 16

Recommended Reading

Banking

Capital City – London as a Financial Centre, Hamish McRae and Frances Cairncross (Methuen), a general introduction to banking institutions, and the work of the financial services industry.

Banking: The Business, Geoffrey Lipscombe (Pitman Publishing), suggested reading if you wish to learn some theory before starting work, and to prepare yourself for the Banking Certificate examinations.

Investment Banking

Modern Merchant Banking, ed C J J Clay and B S Wheble (Woodhead Faulkner), for students of economics and banking, and for the general reader who wishes to be better informed before starting work with an investment bank.

The various tuition guides produced by the Chartered Institute of Bankers list many books and you should use these bibliographies if you are studying for the Institute's examinations.

Careers Literature

The Bank of England, the English and Scottish clearing banks, some international banks, many of the larger investment banks, and major building societies produce excellent careers literature. Often this is aimed at particular types of applicant (GCSE, A level, graduate), and you should read an organisation's careers literature *and* other documentation such as its annual report to shareholders, or brochure prepared for investors, before an interview. The Chartered Institute of Bankers and the Chartered Institute of Bankers in Scotland produce material on their courses which you might find useful to read before starting work.

The Banking Information Service and the Building Societies Association also produce informative booklets with further case studies which will add to your knowledge of their industries.

Other Relevant Material

Great Answers to Tough Interview Questions, 3rd edition, Martin John Yate (Kogan Page)
How You Can Get That Job, Rebecca Corfield (Kogan Page)
Interviews Made Easy, Mark Parkinson (Kogan Page)
The Job Hunter's Handbook, David Greenwood (Kogan Page)
Preparing Your Own CV, Rebecca Corfield (Kogan Page)